SUCCESS EQUATIONS

SUCCESS
EQUATIONS
a path to living
an emotionally
wealthy life

Dr. SHERRIE
CAMPBELL

NEW YORK

LONDON • NASHVILLE • MELBOURNE • VANCOUVER

SUCCESS EQUATIONS
a path to living an emotionally wealthy life

Published in New York, New York, by Morgan James Publishing. Morgan James is a trademark of Morgan James, LLC. www.MorganJamesPublishing.com

The Morgan James Speakers Group can bring authors to your live event. For more information or to book an event visit The Morgan James Speakers Group at www.TheMorganJamesSpeakersGroup.com.

ISBN 978-1-68350-887-8 paperback
ISBN 978-1-68350-888-5 eBook
Library of Congress Control Number: 2017918631

Cover Design by:
Rachel Lopez
www.r2cdesign.com

Interior Design by:
Bonnie Bushman
The Whole Caboodle Graphic Design

In an effort to support local communities, raise awareness and funds, Morgan James Publishing donates a percentage of all book sales for the life of each book to Habitat for Humanity Peninsula and Greater Williamsburg.

Get involved today! Visit
www.MorganJamesBuilds.com

To my daughter London—you are my Reason in life

Contents

Success Equations:
The Way to Emotional Wealth

All of life is built on patterns. As a psychologist, what I study are patterns of behavior. I analyze the patterns that lead people into emotional health and well-being and which patterns lead people to their destruction. Patterns aren't always clear at first, but the more time I spend with individuals and examine the results of their behavior, I can see what patterns are working in their lives and which are destroying them. Because we are all unique and individual, we manifest patterns in our own ways, but the *results* of patterns—whether positive or negative—are surprisingly consistent. Positive patterns show beneficial results, and negative patterns show destructive results. Therefore, when it comes to success in life, I believe we can follow certain formulas, cultivate them as virtues, and greatly increase our chances at living authentically wealthy lives.

I have put together a series of *success equations* to make the path to living a wealthy life more obtainable and sustainable. It is my belief that most anyone can be rich; we can all make money. However, not all of us, due to our more negative patterns, can become wealthy. When we're wealthy, we have it all. We have love, we have family, we have our physical, emotional, mental, and spiritual health, and we have the financial resources to make all other areas of our lives that much more satisfying.

The success equations in this book can be applied in many ways. Each equation is built to stand on its own; therefore, if you feel at any point along your journey that certain virtues seem not to be as strong in you as they once were, you can go back and choose the success equation that most accurately fits what you're looking to improve. You should know, though, that I wrote this book to present the equations more like a pyramid or hierarchy, with each equation being foundational and interdependent with all the others. In grammar school, we learned addition more easily than we did subtraction. It is that same formula which is easiest for us when we approach life and how to live it well. We prefer to have things added to our lives rather than taken away. For this reason, each success equation will add onto the one below it, and the one below it adds to the equation above it. I am about the least math-minded human when it comes to numbers, but I am an expert at mental and emotional patterns. I live by these equations in my own life and teach them to my patients. The results show continual improvement in all areas of life.

Another reason I built the equations in the form of a hierarchy is for the purpose of security. If we fall from one equation, we do not fall into an abyss. We fall into the formulas below it. Success cannot be sustained through challenge or failure without a strong foundation to fall into and rebuild from. As we have all experienced, success is not a straight, upward shot; it's an undulating, somewhat terrifying, unpredictable roller coaster of continually reinventing ourselves to get where we need to go. These success equations are there to support and nurture you emotionally, no matter where you're at or what you're cultivating in yourself to become. Furthermore, the success equations are not necessarily phases you complete or pass through sequentially. Instead, they are best practiced as ongoing states of mind. An essential part of personal growth is practicing the new mind-sets that will make us feel better until they become a natural part of who we are.

My hierarchy of success equations is loosely based on Abraham Maslow's hierarchy of needs. In 1943, psychologist Abraham Maslow published a theory in the *Psychological Review* that was based on his clinical studies of what motivates human beings to seek fulfillment in all aspects of their lives. His needs-based framework went on to become a model for both personal empowerment and workplace leadership. Maslow's hierarchy embraces the concept that basic needs must first be satisfied before higher, more other-centered goals can be pursued and achieved. He believed we have physiological needs, safety needs, love and belonging needs, esteem needs, and self-actualization needs.

Part 1 of the book focuses on our very basic *biological/physiological* needs. To go anywhere successfully, we must meet these needs before we can achieve our more expansive and other-centered needs. Our basic needs are foundational, and when well cultivated, serve as the launching pad for our personal growth and success. We must establish them first for us to be strong enough to build on them our massive structure of success. The entrepreneurial journey must be equipped with the necessary amounts of strength, energy, toughness, grit, oxygen, nutrition, water, shelter, warmth, sex, and sleep to sustain us. These basic needs provide us and our dreams the required balance and fuel to become successful.

Once our biological/physiological foundation is solid, we start Part 2 of the book. There we explore what Maslow calls needs for *security*. In this phase, we arm our dream or vision with the necessary protections, securities, orders, laws, limits, and stabilities to be successful. To develop the security we're looking for, we must think more psychologically. In this phase, we are more focused on our personal development. We learn about courage and self-trust. The primary task is to practice and develop the fearlessness we need to make mistakes, take risks, and fail, and to recover as wiser, smarter human beings. The smarter we become, the better we execute. The better we execute, the more security we develop. It in this phase that we secure the needs of our heart, finances, resources, mind-set, family, and a strong sense of safety.

As we feel more secure, we move to Part 3 of the book. Here we work on cultivating Maslow's needs for *love and belonging*. It is very difficult for love to grow without a strong foundation of security for love and relationships to build from. According to Maslow, we have deep and innate yearnings for family, affection, relationships, and teamwork and to experience an overall sense of belonging to a community. We desire a sense of inclusion. In this phase, love is the task. Love and belonging contribute to our foundational needs for warmth, sex, and oxygen, while also meeting many of our security needs. The more inclusive our community, the more protected we feel. We feel secure when love is present because we have a place to fall when things are rough and people to celebrate with when things are great. Through love, we also learn what love is not. In this phase, we begin to develop the ability to distinguish between who is real and healthy and who is fake and destructive to our lives. We learn who to let go of and who to keep. Most importantly, love gives us a reason to overcome. We must love what we do so deeply that there is nothing—no amount of failure or challenge—that can destroy the dream we are pursuing.

As we cultivate love and experience what it means to be part of a team, we move to Part 4 of the book, meeting what Maslow calls *esteem* needs, which adds the necessary depth to our personal character. Esteem needs include needs for achievement, recognition, status, increased responsibility, and the development of a good reputation. In this phase, we leave the background roles of life and come to be more of a presence on the frontlines. We feel inspired to start leading and contributing to others. By this point, we have suffered, failed, learned to overcome, kept going, and have remained clear about who we are. We are no longer afraid to be honest with others. Nor are we afraid to receive honest feedback from others. We have developed the cognitive prowess, knowledge, meaning, and self-awareness necessary to be able to govern ourselves well and to help others do the same. The task in this phase is to develop our skills to a level of expertise that people know about us and are interested in our product. More than this, though, we crave for others to be drawn to our character.

As we become more interdependent and inclusive and less self-focused on what we have and don't have, we reach Maslow's final stage of development, which is the need for *self-actualization.* The task in this phase is to deeply know who we are and to use our knowledge to help others. We have developed the maturity to perceive reality with objectivity and can tolerate uncertainty without acting impulsively. We have come to accept ourselves for who we are and others for who they are. We have the security within to be more spontaneous in our thoughts and actions, and we can carry a sense of humor when things don't turn out as we had planned. We have become highly individual and are unafraid to break from the status quo, but we are not defiant. We operate from curiosity and wonder rather than from rebellion. We live and love with a strong sense of commitment and morality. The journey we're on has become geared toward sharing.

At this phase of our development, needs for privacy seem to be more natural. We have come to prefer depth to the superficial, and we choose to have fewer high-quality relationships rather than many superficial ones. We lead from empathy rather than from authority, and we have the self-awareness necessary to listen to our own hearts about what is right or wrong. We work hard and are responsible and therefore have become, and continue to become, increasingly more successful. With a deeper sense of connection to ourselves, we have become profoundly concerned with the welfare of humanity. As we have suffered, we have come to understand many have suffered before us. Our suffering has taught us to appreciate the simplicity and divinity in our more basic life experiences. Our mind-set has become more democratic as we have learned to appreciate all people, good and bad.

We have a depth that only comes from experience. We have suffered deep heartbreak and have questioned life, love, God, our reason for being alive, and the character of other people. It is this suffering that has helped us discover who we are spiritually. We have found the God within—the God that doesn't live in a church, a mosque, a temple, a teepee, or some other structure. We have found the God within our own heart. Because of this discovery, we have become more existential and humanistic in our thinking. Success at this stage is about generating the peak experiences we desire through helping, loving, contributing to, and serving others. In this phase, we discover our full wealth. There is nothing higher than this. Yet, it takes discipline and hard work to sustain it. Emotional wealth is a state of mind we choose to cultivate and live. It is an action, an expression of our character, and the depth of our heart.

When God, fate, or the universe are discussed throughout the success equations, my intention is to be inclusive to each of you. Each of you is unique and important. My intention is to create the room to project your own idea of God, fate, or the universe onto what you are reading. I personally believe each of us is endowed with the magic of a deep and enlightening intelligence that is guiding our every step, softening our more painful growth periods, and pushing us forward into more depth and success.

Let us begin our journey together through the success equations so we may develop and perfect the habits that form and deepen our lives. We will learn to develop the patterns that help guarantee we live a wealthy and enriching life—one we will leave behind feeling as though who we were in this world was important.

Part 1
BASIC NEEDS

All the evidence that we have indicates that it is reasonable to assume in practically every human being, and certainly in almost every newborn baby, that there is an active will toward health, an impulse towards growth, or towards the actualization.

—Abraham Maslow

Every journey starts as an idea, a spark of passion, a hope ... a dream. To give birth to this dream, Maslow identified certain core physiological needs that must first be met and maintained. To perform at our peak, we require healthy air to breath, water to keep our systems hydrated, healthy nutrition to fuel our bodies, and adequate time to rest and sleep. When deficits exist in these four basic requirements, we become incapable of developing any ambition, much less acting on it and achieving our full potential. We cannot succeed if we routinely push ourselves under an oppressive regimen. We end up dehydrated, starved, and exhausted. We must be mindful to develop ourselves before we can expect to have a positive and enduring impact on others. In the beginning, we must put ourselves first.

Vision + Purpose = Personal Legacy

Stay true to yourself, yet always be open to learn. Work hard, and never give up on your dreams, even when nobody else believes they can come true but you. These are not clichés but real tools you need no matter what you do in life to stay focused on your path.

—Phillip Sweet

A dream is a basic need. A dream is as important to the functionality of our life as our breath is to the functioning of our body. If we have no dream to pursue, we have no journey to travel into wholeness, happiness, or wealth.

Each of us generates unique ideas.

An idea turns into a dream, and this dream turns into a tangible vision.

A tangible vision becomes a purpose.

A life lived with purpose becomes a crusade.

Having a dream gives our life the emotional nutrition it needs to thrive. It gives our life the depth, meaning, and significance we crave to feel and experience. Our dream gives us a reason to live.

I have always wanted to educate myself but never performed well on standardized testing. As a result, I held the belief that I wasn't smart enough to get into the postgraduate education I desired. I went through some hard years of extreme self-doubt until I took a vested interest in understanding the way in which I learned best. I realized I was a right-brained (creative, intuitive) person trying to thrive in a left-brained (logical, analytical) educational structure. I noticed that my attention span was shorter than others, and I would tune out in long lectures. I found that if I read the text myself and took my own notes, I performed much better. The act of writing things down seemed to solidify the information I was learning in my head. Instead of trying to be different than I was and more similar to those that I erroneously viewed as smarter than myself, I was able to get around standardized testing with the advent of independent learning or online schooling. I now have a doctoral degree. I passed the same state boards as those who went to schools like the University of Southern California, Stanford, or Berkeley, and I am currently a fairly well-known psychologist. I was the girl who hardly made it through grade school, but now I am one of the top writers for Entreprenuer.com and HuffPost. I have been on GMA and other television stations, I run a thriving practice, and I have a large worldwide Facebook following where I help people for free to cope with relationship challenges.

What made such a huge difference? The greatest thing I did was take an interest in myself. I stopped comparing who I was with others. I looked at what worked for me and held tightly to the vision of what I wanted to achieve. I absolutely refused to give in to self-doubt and other destructive emotions. I may not have been the smartest or most talented person in the room, but I was the hardest working, and I caught up with those who I had viewed as more talented and naturally gifted with intelligence. It is so true that when you have the will, you can find the way.

The start of any dream begins as a choice—the choice to bring our dream to life. That choice must be so firm and deeply felt in our heart that we will do anything to reach our desired experience. Like anything in life, the path to success is never a straight shot up the mountain, void of any challenge. Each day, whether we're experiencing hardship or not, is a day we have the opportunity to make a clear and affirmative statement about who we are and what we want out of our lives.

Being successful is a sport in and of itself. Think of the hours upon hours of training athletes put into developing their skill and maximizing their talent. Lindsey Vonn, the most well decorated female skier in history, has gone through one horrific injury after another. But she has a dream. Her dream is to ski in at least one more Olympic Games. Most at her age and history of serious injuries would have stopped long ago. Not so Lindsey Vonn. She trains in my hometown of Vail, Colorado, and the kind of rehab and training she puts into perfecting herself to achieve her dream is exactly what makes her such a remarkable success. She holds a positive attitude and has developed habits and patterns around not giving up that keep her on top. This is why she is so unique. She is talented, of course. But more importantly, she is committed to her dream and trains for the moments when it is her time to shine.

Do you want to do something extraordinary with your life? Or perhaps you are already pursuing that and want to get to your next highest level. If either is your desire, I believe you possess the willingness and passion to learn from what is written here. This book will guide you into living your life to the absolute fullest. It will help you in the most practical ways to get you realizing and expanding upon your dreams.

The way forward starts with you.

So, right now, *declare your dream, declare your expansion.*

Start living it.

The beginning brings us to our first success equation.

Vision
VISION + Purpose = Personal Legacy

Have you ever driven past a graveyard and thought about how many incredible, life-altering dreams or visions only went as far as six feet under? How about that person who thought about inventing a product that would help fireproof a house but came up with every reason why it couldn't or wouldn't work? Or that athlete who had unconsciously decided that she had reached her peak and quit her sport prematurely? Or the aspiring writer who experienced how hard it is to become traditionally published and instead of continuing to try just gave up? We never want to live our lives wondering what would have been if we would have just committed a little more. You can avoid that type of heartbreak. You can live a life of such fullness that when you pass away, people far and wide will know *you were here*—that there was something incredibly special about you and what you did with your life.

To have such a life, every dream and every goal every day must first begin with the vision of what you want. Dreams are the beginning of the idea. A dream is broad and expansive. As we fine-tune our dream, we start creating a more clearly defined vision. Each goal we set acts as a small step toward making our vision become a reality. We must vision. We have to vision. It is essential to vision. The life we live is all about what we envision. All of life's greatest miracles have developed from the tiniest mustard seed of an idea. If others can do it, I assure you that you can do it.

Think about it: If your parents held the dream of having children, then you too started off as a dream in the minds and hearts of your parents. Even if you were adopted, it is likely that your birth parent(s) held a vision of adopting you into a loving family who would raise you in a warm, loving, and supportive environment that they viewed as better than what they could provide for you themselves. It is also true that you started off as an idea in the parents who adopted you, as they may not have been able to have children of their own. If none of these are your story, as it has not been mine, there are still options for your greatness. I grew up as the family scapegoat in a highly manipulative family environment. I had to let go of my idea of family and their negative ideas of me so I could start a new life on my own. In this type of circumstance, you must come to love and honor yourself in the ways others could not or would not and start dreaming about the vision of the life you want to live. Success is a sweet form of retribution. What all of this means is that all forms of greatness, including the greatness of you, began with a vision.

Coachable Moment

Create the highest, grandest, vision possible for your life. Because, you become what you believe.

—Oprah Winfrey

That's right. You can cast a vision for your life as others have for their life. You can have an incredible life. To create this life—the one you daydream of living—you have to find that place inside you where anything and everything is possible. No one is built without this place.

I believe wholeheartedly that *you* were put on this earth for a reason. You were put here to build, live, and leave your own personal legacy. You are not here to be a carbon copy, lost in the crowd, not brave enough to go after your dream. So get up, suit up, and listen up.

The vision you have for your life is alive with an essence only you can manifest. It is designed by you—by your own brand of hope and possibility. Do not keep it from the rest of us! We want to experience it with you.

I know that if your mind can come up with a vision, then the success of that vision already exists in the Realm of All Possibility. I can guarantee you this: If you can see it in your mind, you can have it in your life. You, my friend, were born to be phenomenal.

Now you may be thinking, *Yeah, right. Everything I have ever envisioned, someone else has already done it.*

Well, here is my answer to that. Whatever your talent is, whatever your idea is, even if it is already out there, it hasn't been done by *you* yet. So no, it has not been done yet if you haven't done it.

When I was researching topic ideas for my doctoral dissertation, I was getting frustrated because it felt like every nook and cranny of life had already been studied and researched. Still, I came up with my idea. My idea may have been only one thin slice different than someone else's, but it became *my* research. I am proud to say I ended up writing one of the best dissertations to go through my institution.

When you have a vision, hold it close to your heart. Stay away from the trap of comparison. There is no one—and I mean absolutely no one—who compares to you. There is no one who can do what you do as *you* would do it. You are your own unique flavor of excellence.

Holding a vision of how amazing our life can be is what life is all about. Feeling complete, feeling powerful, feeling confident, and feeling happy are the most basic desires of a human being. What is life worth if it doesn't feel good? The truth is, we are here to live lives we love. Having a dream gives us something to look forward to. Sean Achor, author of *The Happiness Advantage*, says, "happiness is the joy we feel when striving after our potential." There can be no happiness, nothing to look forward to, nothing worth living for without first having a vision.

Visions give our lives meaning in two different ways: visions can be used for inspiration, and they can be used for prediction. First, our visions inspire us to define who we are. When we have a vision, it stirs something from deep within. We feel inspired to live more than a mundane existence and feel compelled to make something of our lives. We start questioning what we need more of. We all crave to feel good enough, good about who we are, and good about what we're doing. This is why inspiring thoughts and ideas serve to point us in the direction of creating a clear vision of what our lives could be. The large majority of us are inspired towards those things we feel an excited anticipation about. The most precious feeling we all deserve to experience is to feel that we matter, that we have something special and extraordinary to offer this world. When we are inspired to live the higher thoughts of who we want to be and what we want to bring to life, we suddenly have a sense of structure. This structure allows us to more accurately predict the trajectory of our path. Having a vision provides us a target to direct our efforts toward. This is emotionally grounding because a vision provides us with a sense of comfort. We are clear in who we are and where we are in our lives every day. Knowing what we're aiming for makes us feel a sense of security and accomplishment. Aimlessness leads us directly into frustration and depression. With each goal we achieve that brings us closer to what we have envisioned for ourselves, the more inspired we feel and the more predictability our lives continue to have.

Abraham Maslow states, "the story of the human race is the story of men and women selling themselves short." The only way to sell ourselves short is not to have a vision for our life. Our dream gives us the most important thing—direction, which is the second way visions give our lives meaning. Our dream helps us more accurately predict the trajectory of our success. It helps us forecast the changes we will need to make in our life to create the better future we are looking for. Having a dream is the powerful force keeping us in movement and focused on living the dream we want.

We should be bold when we envision the life we want. We must open our mind to the Realm of All Possibility—that limitless place where anything and everything is possible. When looking into this space, we must allow it to give us hope. When we have hope, we are more inspired to work hard to create a better, brighter, happier, and bigger future for ourselves. When we can envision a future that is exponentially better than where we are now, we are more likely to make the changes necessary to get there.

A vision is the strongest force we can invite into our lives. I view it as a form of giving birth. The excitement of starting to live our dream is so intoxicating that it awakens the relentless ambition we need when we're pressed up against the ropes, going toe-to-toe with failures, setbacks, emotional hardships, negative feedback, loss, or personal problems within ourselves. When the idea of our vision is strong enough, it is enough to abate these negative forces by not giving them the power to take us off course.

Coachable Moment

In order to carry a positive action, we must develop a positive vision.

—*Dalai Lama*

How to Build Your Vision

To build our dream, we must have a clear idea of what we want.

So ask yourself questions and write your answers. And I do mean *write*. It's my belief that there is nothing more powerful than placing onto paper what we envision. There's something about taking a real pen and putting it to real paper that will make your vision more tangible, more accessible than simply typing it into a computer. Then write down and be curious about all the possibilities available to you. Here are some questions that can help you:

- How do you see yourself living out the rest of your life?
- How do you envision your health, your wealth, your emotional well-being, your relationships, and your levels of happiness and satisfaction?

Keep in mind that success is not just about money. The beauty about a vision is that anything, and I mean absolutely anything, is possible. Nothing is too much or too hard. Do not sell yourself short. Dream BIG.

If you find you are having a hard time finding clarity, get creative. Open your mind. Even explore the lives of others and the visions they created and accomplished. One great way to do this is to read anything and everything from the local newspaper to history to current business or sports magazines to … well, you get the idea. Information helps us see how other people have generated ideas and brought about changes. Learning this helps us find ways of activating needed changes in ourselves. It's an effective practice to dream about where we see our lives going and to research and learn about others who have gone before us and have taken similar paths.

An enjoyable way to start creating a vision is to lose yourself in daydreaming. Haven't we all caught ourselves gazing out of windows, staring up at the sky or out to the vastness of the ocean and been awe-inspired by how immense this universe really is? There is so much opportunity for us outside of the minutia that bogs us down in daily life. You must allow yourself to surrender to your imaginings. There is an unlimited amount of abundance in this universe pining for us to grab hold of it. To dream, we have to get out of our daily grind and set aside some time for creativity. As we daydream, we must believe that life is abundant with opportunity. Believe me when I say this: God takes great joy in prospering for us. We must come to believe that every intention we set for ourselves becomes blessed with a design for our advancement. When we start to believe in this, we start receiving it. This is why many of us who already on this path use vision boards. It allows us to set intentions for what we want to achieve with the belief that having our intentions "out there" in written form communicates directly to God what it is, in detail, that we want. For instance, when I first submitted the manuscript *Success Equations* to Morgan James Publishing, I placed the letter acknowledging that they had received my book proposal on my vision board and I "gave it to God." Several weeks later, I got the call offering me a publishing contract. I cried. I have been chasing this dream for ten years. According to the laws of attraction, God wants for us what we want, and he will prosper us to get there. All that is required of us is our faith, hard work, and a deep belief that we have the power to achieve whatever it is that we put our heart into. When we live according to these requirements, we receive the type of abundance that signifies that we are living well, feeling well, and earning well.

Knowing who we are gives us clarity on the visions we dream about. Any deeply felt achievement begins with a keen awareness of who we are. When we know our values and beliefs and are clear there is a larger and significant purpose to our existence on this earth, we dream bigger. True satisfaction cannot come from chasing someone else's dreams. We have to know who *we* are and what *we* want. We are all much more than the sum total of other people's opinions of us. The experiences we have in life can only have meaning if we seek to understand them, what they mean to us, and how they impact our idea of who we are and what we want. This is invaluable information to gather when visioning about ideas we want to pursue. Our path to understanding develops as we gain increased levels of self-love and self-awareness. At the end of the day, we will each ultimately be defined by our passions and how we did or did not live them out.

When we pursue the desires of our heart, we live with more freedom, personal expression, and relentless abandon. We get out from under people telling us who to be, how to be, and what to do. When we chase our *own* dream, we experience what it means to live independently and individually. We are much more motivated to achieve goals that are self-chosen because they hold the most meaning for us. Each day becomes another opportunity to provide proof of our existence in this world, to show to others and to feel deeply within ourselves that our lives truly matter. Each goal achieved increases our self-belief that we have what it takes to execute on our ideas and be successful. A very basic need we have as human beings is to experience the solidity and power of *who we are*. If we are not solid in ourselves or our dream, the best we can do is construct a life built upon a flimsy foundation of paper cards. To launch any dream of ours, it has to be done from a strong foundation.

Loving what we do and who we are is foundational to our success. When constructing our vision, we must focus on ideas that provide us with enough inspiration, meaning, love, passion, and purpose to move on it. Our dream has to be backed by the pure and unadulterated commitment to achieve it. We are more likely to succeed at the things we are completely invested in, what we are committed to and passionate about. By the way, passion isn't doled out in quotas. Passion is infinite. We are all capable of being passionate about anything and everything when we choose to pursue what we love. And success isn't all fluff and glory. We will not love every part of our journey, but learning to tolerate and learn from these discomforts is what makes our investment of time and energy worthwhile. We must be willing to do *The All of It* to create a solid enough foundation to build our dream upon.

Bottom line, when we love what we do, nothing will stand in the way of our pursuit of it.

All the elite successes we see in our society from people such as Oprah Winfrey, Bill Gates, the late Walt Disney, and countless others concern individuals who have done the things they wanted to do most, and they earned well through it. To live as these people, we must be committed to channeling our work in a direction where our work adds value to others. Happiness and satisfaction come when our financial worth is a direct reflection of how much value we have added to the lives of other people.

Therefore, we must never place limits on our dreams. Visions and dreams are fluid, so we must allow them to be limitless. When we do not place barriers on our dreams, no matter how wild they may seem at first, the things we can conjure up to achieve will be astounding.

I am a firm believer that if you can dream it, you can achieve it. I am asking you to view yourself as the CEO of your own life. As the CEO, you must have a vision. You must have the ability to see the reality of your today and be able to calculate the changes you need to make to create a tomorrow that can grow, improve, and prosper. You must be able to see the future while being focused on the present. You must use today's vision as a stepping-stone, getting you that much closer to the bigger picture you are striving for. Today, *this very day*, is your most useful day in getting you to your more prosperous tomorrow. A vision is not elusive. A dream is a reality you feel deeply compelled to bring into existence, and it is something you can actually do.

As we create successful visions, we naturally begin to feel full of excitement, optimism, and anticipation for what we are building. All of these positive emotions are vital to creating and maintaining the foundation of our dream. As we see ourselves capable of achieving what we want, the excitement we taste from within is sweeter than honey.

Another benefit to holding and creating a vision for our life is how profoundly we grow as individuals. Anytime we vision, we are stretching our minds, our hearts, and our souls. The more solid we are in ourselves, the more unshakable our success will be as we travel upward. On this basic developmental level of envisioning our possibilities and opportunities, we are exercising our capacities to see beyond our current reality. Creating a vision is tantamount to living the most meaningful and special life we can live. In time, and throughout this book, we will see that our vision has the power to bring us into being physically well, emotionally satisfied, intellectually inspired, financially abundant, corporately successful, and spiritually whole. This is what it means to live our purpose.

Purpose
Vision + PURPOSE = Personal Legacy

A Vision Leads to Our Life's Purpose

Some people may ask, "Why have a life purpose? It's too much pressure. What if I am not meant to leave anything of significance behind? What if I don't want to? Why not just live life as I know it and ignore everything else? Why not chill out and relax until my life comes to its end? Why risk when my success isn't guaranteed?"

In response, I ask: Why not make a difference? Why not live above average? Why not live fulfilled and feeling incredible? Why not be as phenomenal as you can be? Are you afraid of hard, meaningful work? If so, why? From who or where did you learn that you can't achieve or that working hard and making a difference aren't options for you?

A truly meaningful life starts with an idea. When we fall in love with a great idea, fate will push us to follow that path. Our ideas have such incredible potential to impact the world, but we have to really want that. Fulfilling our purpose is the prize, not the money, notoriety, or other accolades. Remember, everything in existence today began with a vision. If we do not have a vision for who we are or for what we want out of love, life, and business, we live from routine, where life is reduced to a daily order of events. There will be no excitement and no direction without something of significance yanking us out of bed in the morning.

Knowing our purpose and how we can apply that purpose to every area of our life is what connects us with our desires, passions, and greatest potentials. Regardless of what is going on in the world around us or in the hardships we face, knowing our purpose helps us embrace and accept why we're doing the things we're doing. Knowing our purpose grounds us in times of chaos, and it is the most important element on the path to wholeness and success. We feel more valuable as a person when we set and achieve our visions and goals. Our purpose gives us the experience of our existence, of our significance, and of what it means to feel proud to be who we are. Each small win we gain gives us a new experience of the depth of what we are each capable of achieving. In order to fully experience the depths of our capabilities, we must develop a strong and willful fear against being average. We must refuse to accept mediocrity.

What Is Your Purpose?

Before I answer what your purpose is, I want to ask a related question: What is the value of having a purpose? Well, having a purpose gives us a solid reason to wake up each morning motivated and inspired to have an experience of *ourselves*. We are God's creation in action. In the human psyche, action equates to happiness and depression to aimlessness. When we get active, we get happy. Having a purpose gives us a rock-hard reason to live and not give up. It gives us a reason to try again and again.

So, what is your purpose?

The greatest opportunity this amazing human life offers is for each of us to have a significant and beneficial impact on others. Maslow and renowned human developmentalist Erik Erikson talk of the importance of our impact on others— knowing that who we are, who we have been, and who we are still capable of becoming have held and will hold a positive and lasting influence on the lives of other people. Steve Jobs, for example, will impact this world for eternity. It is through the vision he created at Apple that his memory and influence only continue to grow bigger. It is also our purpose that sets us up to have influence long after we pass.

It is only when we feel we have a purpose in this world that true intentional living begins. When we become *purpose-driven,* we know what we stand for. However, this doesn't make life problem-free. In fact, it may increase the challenges we face because having a purpose comes with great responsibility. The most magical thing about having a purpose is that it gives us our *Reason.* We have the excitement and security of knowing the *Reason* we were put on this earth, and we can use this *Reason* as our living compass.

Purpose brings us into a commitment, and commitment brings us direction and clarity—two things we need to be successful. When we fully commit to anything in our lives, it wipes out any and all meandering. Knowing our purpose helps us differentiate between knowing what is important and what is not. The reality is that most of us are lost doing a million things, which ultimately do not make a difference in our lives or in the lives of others. We internally yell at ourselves to earn more money, buy a new home, or get a new car to be sure we can keep up with the Kardashians. However, all of this chatter has nothing to do with our purpose. When we have a purpose, we know our *Reason.* We are no longer infected or pressured to live these superficial, societal goals that hold little to no meaning. Our purpose cuts directly through the superficial. When we are *purpose-driven,* we focus on what truly matters when it comes to living the dream of our higher existence.

When I talk about living your higher existence, I'm referring to a critical choice you make—the choice to live and contribute in ways that serve to raise your own levels of joy and happiness. As you succeed and experience what you're capable of, your purpose will soon become one that helps others succeed and grow. *You* have this type of power. Never allow yourself to live a random life experience. Strive to have an impact. Strive to live boldly and to experience life to its very depths. To help you, surround yourself with people who are compatible with you and your goals. If you live from a random existence, you cannot live the life you dream of. The destiny that results from your original vision, that leads you to your purpose, is to live a life you can deeply enjoy and love.

I am going to say it again: *You* were put on this earth for a *Reason*. Your mind is capable of visioning, and your body capable of action. In this life, happiness and fulfillment are a byproduct of achievement, so you must work. Since you must work, make sure to work doing what you love. Since you must work, work to grow yourself and to benefit others. Your life can only be as extraordinary as the number of people you impact, help, and inspire. Do not be driven in life by guilt or fear. The ultimate goal is to live for something larger than yourself. When you are purpose-driven, you understand that you are not what you have; instead, you are what you contribute.

Live Your Life on Purpose

To live our lives on purpose, we must live fiercely. This is where we put action behind our dream. We can never make the mistake of assuming that we as people, our lives, or our businesses will grow by osmosis. Just because time goes by in life doesn't somehow automatically equate to the idea that we are also growing or improving as time moves forward. Time doesn't grow things or people; intention backed with action does. It takes focus to live an empowered life. It takes conscious intent to live our lives on purpose. Those who have made the most significant differences in our world are those who have been the most deliberate in living their dream.

If you want your life to have an impact, you must focus that mind of yours. Narrow your focus to the vision of yourself that you want, believe, and trust you can be. You must release justification, excuse making, fear, blame, stress, guilt, and all other emotions that do not serve your purpose. When you are intentional in your actions, you stop waiting to become the person you want to become, and you start being the person you have always wanted to be. No person or business expands by luck or accident. In any given moment in life, you have two options: step forward into growth or step back into the familiar. True success doesn't happen by waiting or staying safe. You must get real and forecast a plan for your personal expansion.

What is a personal expansion plan? Whenever we start something new, we never really know how we are going to accomplish what we want to accomplish. This is when confusion and doubt step in. Creating an expansion plan helps ward off these two nasty, deceitful, tricky, emotional predators. When we are clear in vision and purpose, we have the stability of knowing what we want. When we know what we want, all the world will respond back to us with increased opportunity. When we deeply know what we want and have the fortitude to remain committed to what we believe our purpose to be, there will be no obstacle strong enough to pull us away from what we desire. In fact, challenge and facing the loss of our purpose, in many cases, only draws us deeper into our commitment to stay the course. The thought of losing a purpose we love can only reinvoke our passion to achieve it.

The direction we desire falls into place once our purpose is clear. Clarity helps us plan our growth deliberately. It is up to us to decide where we need and want to grow and go. As we set our goals, we must also set the pace for their achievement. We must be courageous enough to stretch ourselves and place our feet down upon the road less traveled. To live our answers, we must ask the questions necessary to become a person capable of accomplishing the big life and business goals we set. There is truly nothing more fierce, fabulous, or inspiring than individuals who are willing to jump off the cliff of self-doubt and sail into their own success.

I am blessed to have been in the presence of an eighty-six-year-old man who was an MD psychiatrist at a Women of Resilience Conference in Santa Fe where I was speaking. He was taking on a new adventure in his life to become a playwriter on the topic of Emily Dickenson and her poetry. As I watched him, listened to his poetry and to what he was teaching us about resilience through Dickenson, I couldn't help but sit in amazement that at eighty-six he was taking on a whole new adventure in his life. I was so inspired. He was still willing to risk, willing to do something completely new, and to work hard when many people his age would not be. He was not waiting on death. He was seizing every moment of his life. Being in his presence taught me that life only ends—that our dreams only end—when we choose to stop growing. My goal is to be like him when I am his age: still learning, still growing, still risking, and still giving something helpful and meaningful back to this world.

Coachable Moment

And, when you want something, all the universe conspires in helping you to achieve it.

—*Paulo Coelho*

Personal Legacy

Vision + Purpose = PERSONAL LEGACY

The purpose of our life is to feel a sense of our own significance in this world. Our unique legacy will be who we are, how we have made other people feel, and what we leave behind. To live this, to do this, to accomplish this, we must dream—we must vision. And we must be dogged in our pursuit of our vision by living our lives on purpose.

The need for achievement is a core basic need. The dream is the starting place. But without achievement, there can be no happiness, acknowledgement, or impact. When we have a dream, we become powerful. We become powerful enough to risk, which puts us into a direct, engaging, and flirtatious relationship with our own potential. This is why having a purpose makes our life so interesting. We come to learn that whatever we love and give our time and attention to is what creates the legacy we want to live and leave in this world. Love has to be involved. When we love something, we feel inspired to become better than the person we were yesterday. When love is involved, we live with greater intention. As we commit ourselves to our own betterment, everything around us becomes better as a result. When we hold our visions close and love them with all of our heart, our purpose expands and grows.

Our legacy is created as we stop telling other people how to live their lives and we simply focus on perfecting our own. As we get in touch with the essence of who we are and our *Reason* for being here, we come to know that our purpose is wherever our heart is; it is in our heart that we will find our treasure. And if we instead give in to our fears, we will not be able to talk to our heart.

Coachable Moment
The path to heaven runs through miles of clouded hell.
—*Imagine Dragons*

What we crave to feel as human beings is all the happiness, success, joy, goodness, comfort, and security that come from being in the active pursuit of reaching for our goals and living our dreams. We feel the most liberated, powerful, and loved when we are actively striving to make something incredible happen. Therefore, the fulfillment we crave to experience is not in the destination. We must not strive for endings. We must strive to create new beginning after new beginning. Each new destination we successfully reach will become an open door for another new beginning. The most generous gift life offers us is this: We can open as many new doors as we choose. Success and happiness do not stop unless we stop pursuing them.

In the movie *Jerry McGuire*, Cuba Gooding Jr. shouts to Tom Cruise, "I have no heart? I am all heart!"

Live a life you love. Isn't that what you are really alive for? To feel and to have an impact, to make a difference? To know that you're enough and that you matter?

You can only know your significance through the impact you have on others.

Your destiny is the experience of your wholeness as a person, achieved through the journey of manifesting your vision and purpose.

There is no ending.

What do you want your role in history to be? To be able to answer this question and live out the answer, you must have the fitness to take action for what you love.

MARINATE ON THIS

No matter what he does, every person on earth plays a central role in the history of the world. And normally he doesn't know it.

—*Paulo Coelho*

Fitness + Tough-Mindedness = Peak Performance

Take care of your body. It's the only place you have to live.
—Jim Rohn

Our dream, our vision, and our purpose make up the base of our foundation. To construct our dream into a strong and valued legacy, we need durability and energy. We need to put some muscle behind our dream.

In the last equation, we learned that to start any type of movement toward love, success, or happiness, we need to start at the base. To be fully ready, trained, and prepared to take our journey, we must have the health and fitness necessary to move on it. In almost all cases, success largely comes down to grit more than talent or genius. Making a conscious choice to nurture and strengthen our physical body helps train us to push past our limits and to prove to ourselves that we are much stronger than we may think. Being fit and healthy are at the very foundation of our success, and yet many of us neglect our bodies, our brains, our sleep, and even our nutrition.

As a competitive athlete for my entire life, I am certain that my physical fitness is a huge contributor to my business success, my emotional health, my mental well-being, and my spiritual health. Fitness trains me to push my mental and emotional body past what I think I am capable of. When I am "in the zone," I feel incredibly connected to my spirit. I am instantly in touch with the unlimited capacity I have to succeed at anything I put my effort toward. Keep in mind that you can't be great at anything if you aren't willing to commit to it and train for it.

My Peloton spin coach shouts to us as we're all about to pass out: "Don't stop! Take it to the top! … Feel good, look good, do better!"

When you picture successful people, what images do you conjure up? The majority of us will picture someone who is fit, trim, well dressed, full of energy, and ready to roll. Beyond the images, the simple truth is that when we feel good and look good, we *do better*. When we take care of our foundational needs, we work smarter, not just harder.

In the arena of fitness, our personal health training begins. As we seek to fulfill our foundational needs, it is imperative we have the physical, emotional, mental, and spiritual fitness necessary to make it to the top. This is what our next success equation focuses on.

FITNESS + Tough-Mindedness = Peak Performance

Physical Fitness

Success is about wholeness, and wholeness is about loving yourself. Let those last two words sink in: loving yourself. Ask yourself: If you saw your child, wife, or friend upset or somehow not feeling well, would you encourage them to binge on fattening food, drink excessive amounts of alcohol, or develop other unhealthy habits as a way to teach them to cope or solve their problems? Wouldn't you show care to them in different, more productive ways? If so, why then would you treat *yourself* with any less love or respect? If you want those you love to be healthy and to make healthy decisions, why would you allow yourself such a lack of your own love or care?

We are whole people, with many parts to manage each day. If we lack in one area of our health, we compromise another. Our physical health is the foundation of our well-being and must be our number one focus if we are truly dedicated to getting to where we want to go.

I look at health this way: Imagine a triangle with the base labeled *physical*, above that is the *emotional*, above the emotional is the *mental*, and above that the *spiritual*, with each level totally dependent on the levels underneath. To be healthy emotionally, mentally, and spiritually, you must have the solid foundation of physical health and wellness necessary to achieve wellness on the other levels. Truly successful people understand that there is a direct correlation between good health, fitness, and success. The majority of successful people have a daily routine surrounding their physical health. Most start or end their days with a burst of energy and the feel-good endorphins that fitness offers.

Many of us hold as one of our main priorities to maintain or obtain the position of one of the top performers in our field, company, or industry. This focus is a great motivator, and it takes more than just simple desire to achieve it. We can only grow in our business as much as we grow ourselves. To be the top performer, run a leading company, get a book published, finish our education,  or achieve anything else of high value in our lives, we have to approach it from a perspective of wellness. If we're not physically healthy, we may be able to maintain our peak performance levels for a short time, but ultimately we will burn bright and fizzle fast. We must start thinking about our health and how we can incorporate daily rituals to create levels of well-being that support us to function at our optimal levels of performance.

Fitness and Success

There is an undeniable link between improved fitness and increased productivity. Fitness enhances our ability to solve problems, it increases stamina and energy, and it reduces feelings of stress and fatigue. It also teaches us that we can push ourselves beyond thresholds we did not think were possible. Fitness, as a side effect, trains in the habit of following through and hanging in there when things get tough. Fitness goes far beyond looking good as well; yet, looking good is also extremely important. Whether we like it or not, whether it is fair or not, we naturally judge a book by its cover. We have to admit that when we feel good about how we look, we increase in charisma and confidence because we feel proud about who we are. If we don't take care of ourselves, people will naturally and unconsciously not take us as seriously. We will be seen as less intelligent, lazy, noncommittal, low on self-love, worn out, and less competent in our ability to meet the required needs and standards expected of us.

Coachable Moment

I hated every minute of training, but I said, "Don't quit. Suffer now and live the rest of your life as a champion."

—*Mohammed Ali*

Nutrition and Success

Aside from exercise, eating habits are a huge part of our foundational needs. How many times have we all heard "We are what we eat"? The facts show that good nutrition is absolutely necessary to sustain life and prevent the onset of aging diseases. If we choose to eat unhealthy, we will be unhealthy.

When it comes to unhealthy eating, it takes zero thought or effort to eat quick, fattening, accessible, processed food. Because health begins from the inside out, wellness is largely accomplished through what we eat. Making wise decisions when it comes to food is critical to us consuming the vitamins and minerals necessary for our brains and bodies to perform at the optimal levels we desire.

Did you know that when we feel hungry, most of the time we are actually thirsty? We must hydrate. And when we do, it's even more beneficial to add lemon to water for its surprising health benefits. Lemon water is a great substitute for morning coffee. Although lemons do not contain caffeine, they have excellent pick-me-up properties without the negative side effects. (I read somewhere that it takes six liters of alkalized water to balance out the acidity of one cup of coffee in the body. Yikes!) Lemon water energizes the brain, especially if it is warm, and it hydrates the lymph system. One of the most important benefits of lemon water is its strong antibacterial, antiviral, and immune-boosting power, making sick days from work nearly nonexistent. Lemon water cures headaches, freshens breath, cleanses the skin, improves digestion, eliminates PMS (yes ladies, it's true, so stop with those water pills!) with its diuretic properties, and reduces acidity in the body. Most importantly, lemon water increases cognitive capacity and improves mood with its stimulating properties on the brain, helping us operate more consistently in our peak performance zones.

When we are fit with healthy eating habits, we live with an unbounded energy to work to live our dreams. With the competition in the business world consistently increasing, employees who miss fewer days of work are largely favored and rewarded. Eating clean helps us create, feel, and sustain a healthy body and a positive mental attitude. A positive mental attitude is one of the greatest predictors of success and overall happiness. Stated another way, the health of our body is the ultimate weapon against our competition. A properly fueled entrepreneur will be ready to negotiate, fight, and win.

Sleep and Success

The mental prowess we need to depend on is hugely affected when we fail to get enough sleep. Our ability to function on all levels is deeply compromised as well. When we sleep, the brain gets a relaxation bath, where it rids itself of the accumulated metabolic waste between cells and neurons. When we sleep, the space between our cells increases, allowing any waste between them to freely empty out. It is imperative to our overall functioning that we give our brains this nightly flush.

It is well known that the average person needs six to eight hours of sleep. Depriving ourselves of even an hour each night has cumulative effects powerful enough to negatively impact our mental dexterity all week long. When we lack sleep, we experience lower emotional thresholds; we decrease in focus, concentration, reasoning, and memory; we demonstrate increases in anxiety, frustration, impatience, and depression, which often leads us to indulge in overeating or indulging in other quick fixes such as coffee—anything to try to keep us going. Furthermore, when we're exhausted, we tend to skip our daily workout. Clearly, when we are not getting enough sleep, we are operating far below our optimum.

Coachable Moment

I studied, I met with medical doctors, scientists, and I'm here to tell you that the way to a more productive, more inspired, more joyful life is getting enough sleep. Sleep your way to the top!

—*Arianna Huffington*

Emotional Fitness

To be emotionally well, we must be physically fit and getting the proper amount of sleep. Emotional balance is near to impossible for any of us to manage if we're not healthy. Being physically healthy and well rested are two elements that give us a head start on emotional management.

Each of us has our unique emotional temperament and unique emotional past. We have traveled our own individual journey throughout our lives. Still, we share a wide array of emotions, such as joy and pain. To be successful, we must be able to harness and manage our emotions well, not solely in our professional lives but also and especially in our personal lives. If our personal lives are full of chaos and drama, it is much more difficult to work at our peak performance.

When we're emotionally out of control, we have a tendency to be extremely controlling, to lose our temper, get less sleep, eat impulsively, offend others, and compromise our position through the abuse of our authority. People won't enjoy being around us, working for us, or with us. Human emotions are known for their distorting power. They distort reality, blocking us from seeing the bigger picture with any clarity. Explosive emotions are obviously not the winning formula for our success, longevity, or happiness. In fact, the greatest psychological predictor of heart attack is anger. Practicing emotional intelligence or mindfulness increases our ability to harness our emotions, allowing us to lead more successful and fulfilling lives.

If you struggle with managing your emotions, I urge you to read at least one of these books: *The Anger Trap*, by Les Carter, and *Emotional Intelligence 2.0*, by Travis Bradberry. In the meantime, here is the counsel I give to my patients when it comes to handling their more chaotic emotions. You need to lean back and flow with whatever you are feeling without having to act out of your emotions. Give your emotions the space and time to rise and fall. Anxiety makes you feel as if there is an imminent emergency. You may believe that if certain tasks or conversations aren't resolved immediately that you will face horrific, negative outcomes. In rare cases, this may be true, but most things turn out for the best when they are given a little time to settle. When you operate with emotional maturity, you are better able to recognize your emotions, label them, and remain self-possessed. When you can hold onto yourself, it allows you to listen to others and take in information that may help you mitigate the emotions that are flooding you. When you listen and remain calm, it allows you to operate from the facts rather than from distortion and embellishment. When you can roll with whatever you're feeling, gather information, remain calm, and think clearly, you set yourself up to make excellent decisions. Good decision-making leads you toward increased success while also keeping your important relationships intact instead of blowing them up with an emotional-laden outburst.

I used to be plagued with worry and profound fears of the future. When life would bring me the unexpected, I was unable to respond with the emotional maturity that I wanted. Instead of being able to see my situation objectively, I would panic, lose sleep, lose my appetite, overthink, and paralyze my decision-making process. As I have worked on trusting myself, I have become more adaptable to life's challenges. It's not that I don't panic anymore, because I do. But now I recognize when I am in panic-mode and know this is not the time to make decisions. I have trained myself to wait and hold on until the right answers come. And they do come. Moreover, my worst-case scenarios almost never happen. One the most effective tools I use to help me wait is writing down the thoughts that cause my panic. Writing puts my thoughts in perspective, and it's where solutions to my problems seem to more naturally arise. I have written my way through my terrors into triumph time and again. When I write, maturity is almost always present because the act of writing slows me down and helps me connect with my more rational and objective mind.

Because emotions are contagious, we must surround ourselves with positive emotional supports. There is nothing more important to our emotional health than feeling loved and knowing we belong to a larger community of support. Healthy, loving relationships increase our happiness, success, and longevity, and they promote our capacity to function in life as our best self. Why be anything less than our best? Social connectedness and love gift us relationships to be motivated for and people to be inspired by. How beautiful is that?

When we live in the beauty of feeling genuinely loved and loving, life is abundant. We make sure to carve out the quality time necessary to nurture our important relationships. Having these connections serves to decrease feelings of isolation, loneliness, and self-hate. When we feel deeply loved, we feel exalted. No other emotion has this type of power. Love is God's language. It makes us feel confident enough to get out in the world motivated to live our dreams to the fullest. It pushes us to change. When love is involved, we are inspired to dig deeper into ourselves in an effort to prove our worth even further to those we value most. We are also more willing to explore our potential. Whenever and wherever we feel loved and supported, we become more daring to take the risks necessary for our increased growth and success. Success is always on the edge of that risk; therefore, success is better accomplished when we feel the love of others backing our efforts.

To be healthy emotionally, we need love just as much as we need good nutrition, good sleep, and a great workout.

Coachable Moment

A deep sense of love and belonging is an irreducible need of all people. We are biologically, cognitively, physically, and spiritually wired to love, to be loved, and to belong. When those needs are not met, we don't function as we were meant to. We break. We fall apart. We numb. We ache. We hurt others. We get sick.

—*Brené Brown*

Mental Fitness

The mind is perhaps the most difficult level of our triangle to control. The world of thought is often erratic, negativistic, and largely not under our control. The mind has one essential need: discipline. We must train ourselves to adopt a flexible, firm, yet positive mind-set. All dreams will face their do-or-die moments in the realm of thought.

The detrimental effects of negative thinking patterns are incredibly deceitful and harmful to the mind, body, and spirit. If we give our negative thoughts the power to run our lives, we will run ourselves into the ground. We must train our minds not to talk *about* our problems but to talk *to* our problems.

When we talk *to* our problems, it turns our problems into something external to us that can be seen from a more objective point of view.

When we talk *about* our problems, they remain unseen, undefined, and inside of us where we have little access to establishing objective control over them.

An effective way to talk *to* our problems is to write down our fears or concerns, and begin taking the steps of working ourselves toward solutions.

Talking *about* our problems is essentially complaining. It is not possible to complain ourselves into solutions. It is one thing to feel stressed, but we want to be mindful to avoid stressing over our own stress. When we talk about our problems, we only find more problems.

However, when we talk *to* our problems, we disrupt the negative thinking pattern we're in, creating the room for us to ask the questions that will pull us into solutions.

When I am being challenged, I have made it a habit to see my problem as my partner. I ask my problem questions. I ask what I can do with this problem rather than how I can get rid of it. And I try to predict what all the varying solutions to my problem could be. I take note of those answers and prioritize which outcomes would provide me with what I most desire to happen. Then I begin working my way toward the solution. Approaching my challenges in this way pulls me out of complaining and puts me in the interactive process of dialoguing with my challenges and all of their possible solutions. Talking about my problems keeps my problems alive and without solution, but when I talk to them, the process is more hopeful, interactive, creative, and effective.

Coachable Moment

Nothing can stop the man with the right mental attitude from achieving his goal; nothing on earth can help the man with the wrong mental attitude.

— *Thomas Jefferson*

What is the trick to keeping our mind-set upbeat? Consistently feed the brain positive, motivating, and success-driven information. Audio books are a great way to keep ourselves positive. Many of us spend a tremendous amount of time in our cars or using mass transit to travel to and from work. We must utilize this time to develop a positive mind-set. There are also mindfulness apps, such as *Think Up*, to help us do this. A mind empty of new knowledge and information will go negative immediately. Keep in mind that negative thinking is languid and takes zero effort, while to develop a positive focus, we must manage our minds. The state of our mind is the key to our success. As the famous saying puts it, "Whether you think you can or you can't, you are correct."

If you want to build and sustain the success you're looking for, there are many ways to do this. You can reach out to community by going to church or attending seminars, or you could invest in hiring a business coach or a therapist. Whenever you involve yourself in a community, even if it is a community of two, you open yourself up to new insights and perspectives. When you open your mind in this way, not only do you learn something new but you also find solutions you may not have been able to generate on your own. Another way to access community support is to go directly to your team. Have people on your team who keep you grounded, inspired, and emotionally crisp.

Growing ourselves can also be done in a solitary fashion. There is no greater gift to give yourself than to read, read, read. Get your hands on material that directly relates to the areas where you desire growth. The more you read, the more you learn, and the more confident you become. As they say, "knowledge is power."

Success, at the highest levels, is never a one-person job. Keep your mind busy and goal oriented. Let there be no room for the negativity that will impede your climb to the top. Your mind is under your control. It is up to you to harness your power over it. All it takes is putting some conscious effort into thinking about your own thinking. When you find yourself feeling or thinking negatively, reach for the support that can redirect you in a more positive direction.

The mind is the most powerful instrument we have when it comes to succeeding or failing. It is either our best friend or our worst enemy. It is the one enemy that is more powerful than all others. Our mind can turn on us in a nanosecond if left unmanaged. We cannot allow ourselves to believe our negative, fixed, fear-based thoughts. They are no more mature than that of a two-year-old. They lie, distort, convince, and manipulate us. When our thoughts are out of control and we become aware of it, we must kick them out of the driver's seat and reroute them to believing in what we're doing, working hard for, and succeeding in.

Coachable Moment

People with a growth mindset believe that they can improve with effort. They outperform those with a fixed mindset, even when they have a lower

IQ, because they embrace challenges, treating them as opportunities to
learn something new.

—*Travis Bradberry*

Spiritual Fitness

When we are fulfilled physically, emotionally, and mentally, that in and of itself
is a spiritual experience. It means we are in tune with the moment, with the flow
of life, and with the bigger purpose we have the potential to live. Truly successful
people make time in their daily lives to connect with their spirit. It is within
our spirit that we embody that Creative Intelligence that powers our life. The
divine plan for all of us is one of freedom. Bondage is not God-ordained. We
each intrinsically know that freedom is our birthright, which is why we crave to
dream, to vision, and to know our *unique* purpose. We are each here to express
ourselves as vastly and divinely as we can as the powerful, individual person we
each have the potential to be. The choice is ours.

Making the best choice requires that we self-connect—a powerful step that
catapults us forward in incredible ways. Time in your own company connects you
(with your idea) of God. All your creativity is born from this relationship. You
have been made individual for the purpose of expressing and experiencing your
own God-given creative power. Give yourself permission to take the pressure off,
to temporarily disconnect from your stress, and to get in touch with your spirit.
Alone time allows you to have conversations with your creative self. It gives you
the space and time to analyze what is going well in your life, what you want to
do more of, and the things you want to change. When you gain the insights that
come from this experience and apply them, they will undoubtedly elevate and
improve the quality of your life. When you're connected to your creative power,
you radiate. Your inner beauty and positive energy soothe all those whose lives
you touch. Others get the sense you have tapped into something special that
makes you stand out. As you grow, so do your depth and wisdom, your success,
and your notion of God. As your ideas of God grow, you are given more to give

to others. This is the gift. The healthier you are, the more you have to share. Being able to live from this deep of a well feels absolutely incredible. This is what it means to live a life fulfilled.

To summarize, we must be fit on all levels to experience the creative growth of our spirit. The greatest reward to come from physical fitness is increased productivity and focus. Believe it or not, our physical bodies are similar to machines. If we do not take care of our physical body, it will breakdown. It is essential to our success, happiness, and longevity that we take the necessary steps to care for ourselves. Physical exercise, along with sound nutrition, rev up our mental sharpness, enhance our efficiency, elevate our mood, and help us better manage stress. The result is an overall feeling of strength and well-being. I can nearly guarantee that as your fitness levels increase, so will your position on the ladder of success.

The more physically fit we are, the more control we have in managing our emotions and thought patterns. The greatest gift to come from a positive mind-set is an overall feeling of hope and happiness. The more we train our mind to believe we can attain higher levels of success, the more intentionally we come to live our lives. The more intentional we are in living our lives, the more control we gain over our environment.

I encourage you to purposefully choose your mind-set as a way to prophesy your day. To prophesy means to have some level of predictive power over how your day will turn out. There is not a more spiritual experience than being disciplined and living your life healthfully, effectively, and mindfully. When you feel free to express who you are and see how being who you are positively impacts the world, it gives you a sense of the power of your own spirit. So often in my life I catch myself letting my life live me. In other words, I catch myself feeling victimized by or at the mercy of my life, feeling as if I have very little choice or control. This has never made me more productive. I have become aware that I am the only person who can get me to "better." I get to better by waking up and choosing how I want my day to go. I list out what needs to be accomplished and then schedule my tasks. This provides me with a sense of power and predictability over my circumstances, where life is the car and I am the driver.

Keep in mind that anything that requires discipline is a spiritual practice. Your spiritual fitness is cultivated from the disciplines of being physically, emotionally, and mentally healthy. When you are disciplined on these levels, the creative power you have is unlimited.

Tough-Mindedness

Fitness + TOUGH-MINDEDNESS = Peak Performance

What does it mean to be tough-minded? It means we dig deep into the grittiness we need to pull from to continue on—no matter the obstacles we face.

Take a moment, right now, for just one heartfelt, grounding, deep breath. Open your mind. *You* have the grit I'm talking about. We *all* have it. It exists at your very core. You were designed for survival. If you reach deep enough, you will find the power you need to stay the course.

Grit is defined by how hard you're willing to work without giving up. It is this grittiness that allows you to be persistent and resilient in the face of failure, loss, success, and challenge. It keeps you committed. The successful utilize grit while the fearful don't dig deep enough to find it.

Ask yourself, *Who am I going to be?* Are you going to be gritty, tough-minded? To be tough-minded you must make sure that whatever you pursue gets nothing less than your full and persistent attention. It means there is no amount of hard work you will shy away from if it means losing an opportunity. Because of this commitment, you are sure to resist the temptation to slack. You must commit to staying focused and determined and 100 percent resolute in the pursuit of your goals. I have lived this way every day of my life, and my grittiness has never, even once, failed me.

To consistently do what needs to be done with a laser focus and an unshakable commitment is incredibly difficult for most people. Succeeding requires learning how to get back up and keep going through all failure and adversity. This ability to get back up is a practiced and well-honed trait in the tough-minded, and one we must each adopt to reach the levels of success and satisfaction we crave. It doesn't matter how talented or genius we are if we cannot get up and keep going after a failure. If we are to be tough-minded, we need to kick the inner martyr out of our self-talk. History is our most valuable teacher. Once we get the lesson, we must not allow ourselves to harbor any pain or embarrassment. We must train ourselves to let our mistakes go and move on.

Bottom line? We do better when we know better. We learn what not to dwell on. We also learn how to make sure that we and those we're around get things exactly right moving forward.

Coachable Moment

Nothing in life has happened to you. It's happened for you. Every disappointment. Every wrong. Even every closed door has helped make you into who you are.

—Joel Osteen

We must view succeeding as something that is largely under our own control. To be tough-minded, we cannot think about, wait for, wish for, or depend on luck. Luck has very little to do with success or failure. Luck is something we create through perseverance, a positive mental attitude, and networking for opportunities. "Luck" is really the gift of never giving up. Like the Cowardly Lion from the Wizard of OZ said, "If you stay on the merry-go-round long enough, you're bound to catch the brass ring." Tough-minded successes do not come about through luck. When we're tough-minded, we know when we succeed that we caused it and when we have failed that we caused it. Taking ownership of our failures and successes is much more useful than worrying about when or if luck will strike. It's simple: We must work hard, stay committed to our dream, and create the space for things to fall naturally into place.

To toughen up our mind, we must refuse to entertain any thoughts of lack. Rather than feeling insecure about the success of others, we must shift our attitude into being supportive and excited for what they have achieved. When we come from insecurity, we hold the false belief that there is only so much success to go around, so when someone else takes the stage, we are prone to erroneously believe that their success is somehow reflective of our lack of it. We must learn to support the success of others and to spend the majority of our time around those who are as successful, if not more successful, than ourselves. In reality, our success can only increase in being influenced and inspired by the successful others we spend our time with.

My advice to you is this: Only speak in terms of success. Make no time for "poor me," complaining, whining, or martyring about how things are so bad in your life. Words have power. Language is life. What you speak about is what you live. Complaining has never proven to make people feel better or to become more successful. If there is a failure, be tough-minded and find a way to turn it into a success. Focus on solutions, not problems. If you are going to be competitive, be competitive with yourself. It is wasteful to be competitive with others, over what others have, their job titles, or their accomplishments. When you focus on comparing yourself to others, you diminish yourself.

I will say it again: if it hasn't been done by *you*, then it hasn't been done yet. There is no need to one-up another person. To be tough-minded, remain goal-oriented but only compete with yourself and the goals you set. Each goal achieved is a competition won. To compete with others breeds low-level emotions, such as envy or resentment. If you waste time in these traps of comparison, you weaken your state of mind and the perception you hold of yourself.

To train ourselves into tough-mindedness, we must put our responsibilities first. We must be willing to delay gratification by placing our leisure activities on the backburner until we have cleared our plate of the significant tasks we need to complete. With this winning formula, our success is nearly guaranteed. Succeeding is all about consistency and putting in the time and effort necessary to do what needs to be done.

These are simple principles, and when utilized, we set ourselves up to live our dream. This winning formula of simple and practical principles will prove time and again that our successes are always much more rewarding than our times of laziness, procrastination, and a lack of responsibility.

Peak Performance

Physical Health + Tough-Mindedness = PEAK PERFORMANCE

The commitment we make to our lives physically, emotionally, mentally, and spiritually allows us to perform consistently at our peak performance levels. Our spirits get tired when we're engaged in constant activity. It is a necessary pick-me-up on all levels to engage in some type of physical activity each day. To be successful at the highest levels, we must never underestimate the value of good nutrition, exercise, and rest. Our brain is the most efficient computer. It's ability to stay virus-free and functioning at optional levels is directly affected by what we put into our body, the chemicals we release through exercise, and the restorative powers of sleep. When we take care of our health, we are supplied with the necessary energy and focus for building our wealth personally, professionally, and spiritually.

Critical to all of this is to strive to be unapologetically optimistic. This is what tough-mindedness is all about. Look for the best in any situation. Find the blessings in your bummers. Commit to being hopeful. Expect that somehow and in some way things are rigged in your favor. Let your hardships become your wisdom teachers. A positive outlook will strengthen your immune system and the emotional quality of your life, allowing you to be resilient in the face of fear, stress, and challenge.

Being an optimist or a pessimist boils down to the way you talk to yourself. When you are optimistic, you are steadfast in the belief that it is your own actions that result in positive things happening. You live by positive affirmation, take responsibility for your own happiness, and anticipate good things to happen in your future. This is the key to your spirit. Optimism is the strongest form of spiritual faith. When bad things happen, do not blame yourself. Instead, be willing to *change* yourself. As you practice living this way, your ability to work at your peak performance levels is guaranteed.

Once we are operating at our peak from our foundation, we start becoming naturally curious about expanding who we are and what we know.

We've built the base.

We have our dream.

We know our purpose.

We have the fitness, tough-mindedness, optimism, and spiritual faith to start that next level of our development—the next level of living our dream.

Because we have strength at our foundation, we can be more confident in the viability of our dream. We have proven to ourselves that we have what it takes to keep improving and striving. Our foundation now has the strength to hold any and all increases in our dream.

MARINATE ON THIS

Make no small plans, for they have no power to stir the soul.

—*Niccolo Machiavelli*

Focus + Flexibility = Advancement

Progress lies not in enhancing what is,
but in advancing toward what will be.
—**Khalil Gibran**

L ife isn't life without progress; yet, progress is largely dictated by readiness and timing. To take flight from our foundation means we are ready to start leaping out and testing the market with our idea. We have the dream, we know our purpose, and we have the fitness, energy, and optimism necessary to start making larger movements forward. When we have these basic formulas in place, we advance.

Our commitment in this phase must be to advance forward a little bit each day. If we are not doing this, we are not succeeding to our potential. Let the thought of advancing be inspiring rather than terrifying. We must trust that what we have established underneath us is solid enough for our dream to take us further outside of our comfort zone.

Keep in mind that it is when we feel the most prepared to advance that we most deeply experience the "approach-avoidance conflict," a well-known conflict in psychology. This psychological conflict occurs when we feel tremendous anxiety the closer we get to taking any real action toward our dream. These actions expose us and our idea to the world. When our dream is far in the distance and we're exploring and training for it, we have no doubt we can achieve what we have set before us. But as we approach closer and closer to taking real action toward our dream, we naturally experience tremendous fears, doubts, and questions about whether we should have further weighed the positive aspects of advancing more heavily than the potential adverse aspects. In other words, the unknowns become larger and more terrifying as we get closer to making things real. This is a healthy and necessary battle to work through. As we work through these types of psychological conflicts, we start learning what's needed to be successful over the long-term.

Bottom line: To advance, to leave our base, we have to leap into the unknown and sink or swim.

This is your time.

Right now.

To advance.

You are more than capable.

Focus

FOCUS + Flexibility = Advancement

Have you ever asked yourself how you feel about hard work? I am one of those people who loves challenging, productive work. I work from my heart rather than from the mind-set of "I have to." Whenever I feel like I have to do something, I feel forced and the motivation isn't there because, for me, pressure kills longing. The mind-set of desiring, of wanting to do the work, makes me look forward to Monday. I work from love. I work from excitement. And I work to make a difference. I work to feel and experience my personal significance. The way I stay focused is through prioritizing the health and direction of my mental well-being.

For you to sustain your success, you will require a deep and dogged commitment along with a detailed and solid plan of action at every new step in your process. You can do this. You can do anything if you want it badly enough.

In this process, I encourage you to listen to your fears but not to host them. Fears act as parasites to your motivation. When you are totally focused on the direction you want to advance, this focus will cut through your confusion and doubt. Expect hardship to be a part of your journey; it will be a traveling partner. View it as your motivator to become even better.

Are you totally committed to your dream?

Can you be flexible in adapting your vision when necessary in order to continue advancing?

Are you willing to do what others aren't for you to be and feel successful in the ways you dream of?

You must be in it to win it, no matter what it takes. You can do it! I know you can. And the great news is that being focused is directly under your control.

Coachable Moment
The only place that success comes before work is in the dictionary.
—Vince Lombardi

Live Words, Not Resolutions

There is no greater asset to success than being mentally healthy and focused.

How we start the morning sets the tone for the rest of the day. We must commit to starting each day with the intention of expecting great things to happen. We must expect to advance. When we wake up on the wrong side of the bed, it sets a negative tone, and it can feel like nothing good will happen for the rest of the day. Negative emotions contaminate our focus and are powerful enough to dominate our entire day if we let them. Commit to starting each day with a positive mind-set since it is nearly impossible to advance from negativity.

Here's what I do. I choose to live a word each year. I live that word throughout every aspect of my day, good or bad, for the entire year. This past year, I chose the word *upgrade*. In that year, I purchased my own home, got a new car, increased my fee for service, hired a business coach, built a home gym in my garage, took Fridays off to write, started juicing each morning for breakfast, and fell in love with a quality man. It was a year of great and exciting change that improved my life immensely, and what helped me was focusing each day on the word *upgrade*.

More often than not, with resolutions, we burn bright and fizzle fast because life gets busy, we get distracted, and we forget what we initially set out to achieve. Our old habits can supersede our well-intentioned resolutions. However, when I live one word and focus on that word instead of on ten different resolutions, I grow in all areas of my life. It is an easier way for me to stay committed and focused.

I challenge you to live words in place of resolutions, and see how much change you manifest. You can live a new word each day, choose a new word each week, or one word for each year. Get creative and see what happens.

Here is a list of some great words to keep you mentally focused and advancing in your personal growth, life, and career:

composure	rich	confident	wise
elegant	self-control	faithful	unhurried
quiet	blessing	poised	fearless
calm	diligent	gracious	hard working
smart	deliberate	blessed	upgrade
honest	inspired	tolerant	rest
healthy	driven	resilient	daring
positive	motivated	abundant	aware
successful	kind	open	loving
discerning	patience	commitment	persistent
fun	thoughtful	supportive	flexible
gratitude	creative	interested	willful

Take the word *commitment* and envision all of what it means. What is the true nature of a committed person? Once that picture becomes clear, become intentional about living as a committed person without procrastination in your every word and action.

To be successful, we must have a pristine focus, where we refrain from skipping steps in any process for the sake of getting ahead. Everything needs to have a beginning, middle, and end. We must commit 100 percent only to the step we're in without the need to push the river. Rivers flow by themselves and do not need to be pushed. Trying to force the flow of life only depletes our energy. It is wiser to go with the flow and enjoy the experience. Brute force isn't nearly as powerful as patience. When we work within life's natural flow versus trying to force issues or results, we're happier and healthier and we enjoy more. The lesson is to accept what is and to commit to working with that. When we make the word *commitment* a verb, an action, we give our full attention to the task at hand all the way through to its completion. A life lived with commitment produces a life of follow-through, which naturally leads to our advancement.

The more committed we are to our vision, the more wholeheartedly we approach achieving it. Laziness gets us nowhere, other than living an average or below average existence. We must be hardnosed to succeed, and to do it with as positive an attitude as we can muster. The most practical way to speed up the process of reaching our goals is committing to do what needs to be done. If we find ourselves waning in motivation, all we have to do is remember that word we are living is *commitment,* and it will be enough to push us that extra mile. It's fairly simple, especially when we love what we do. We commit because we love the work. Money becomes the positive side effect. The word *commitment* is what drives our willingness to work hard.

Coachable Moment

If you're not willing to work hard, let someone else do it. I'd rather be with someone who does a horrible job, but gives 110% than with someone who does a good job and gives 60%.

—*Will Smith*

In reality, we all are born with equal opportunity. Where do we differ? We differ in fortitude, effort, resilience, and the willingness to make our lives what we want.

Let's look at the word *willful*. What does it mean to be *willful*? What would be different about our lives if we lived from the purity of willingness? If we live from willfulness, we live with an open and flexible mind-set to go wherever our journey chooses to take us. We are willing to bend, flex, shift, and change whenever called to do so and all in an effort to continue pursuing our goals. We choose to focus on what we dream of doing instead of shying away from the journey and complaining about the aspects of it that we find less than pleasing. When we're willing, we keep our eyes on our dream so intensely that setbacks do not set us back—instead they repurpose us. If we have willingness, we work late whenever necessary, exercise when we're tired, and do things the hard way when we could slack and make life easier.

Anywhere we are truly focused, our lives will naturally upgrade. Let's look at how to live the word *upgrade*. What does it mean to *upgrade*? *Upgrade* means to be better, to improve, to expect more, to put in the necessary time and effort, to increase our standards, and to rise far above where we currently are. It means we are ready to reach for the next bigger, more exciting, and lucrative level of our potential.

How can we apply the word *upgrade* to every area of our lives? We must ask how we can upgrade in our career, as a husband, wife, father, or mother? How can we upgrade our health or our financial situation? How can we upgrade as a friend, a boss, or an employee? As we envision these upgrades, we must write down what we see and conclude. The actions we need to take to upgrade will fall onto the paper. It is up to us to live what we write out. Our answers will shape and direct how we advance.

To advance, we must also bring the concept of *rest* into our daily routine. How can we daily live the word *rest* and still strive wholeheartedly toward our success? Rest is a basic and necessary need. Without rest, focus cannot be maintained. When we rest, we consciously slow things down and harness the unhealthy habit of frantically hurrying through life. When we contemplate the word *rest*, we will feel ourselves immediately slow down to this moment. We will feel calm, which has the power to calm everyone else and the environment around us. We need to give our body the physiological rest it needs. A tired brain loses its ability to pay attention to detail, leading to errors in our work. Rest means to settle. When we feel overwhelmed with stress, we must remind ourselves to bring it back down to a restful, rational state of mind. We must make ourselves take restful breaks during the day where we can sit for a moment and just breathe, gather ourselves and refocus. We cannot hurry, rush, and think rationally or effectively at the same time.

The journey to success will take time. We need to allow for time. We can't push the river. In this light, contemplate how you can live the word *patience*. What does the word *patience* represent? Isn't it appealing to envision ourselves as more patient? Patience helps orient us to the time and place we are in. It is important to know what is our forecast while being mindful that getting to the future desired results we crave is a process. Succeeding takes time. When we lose patience, more errors in our work are made. We must hold onto ourselves enough to slow down and have faith in the process. We must be mindful that our advancement isn't an event but a process. Almost nothing is an emergency. Things have a natural way of falling into place around what we have already set in motion. When the unexpected surfaces, we must allow patience to replace impulsivity. *With patience and focus, you—yes you—can achieve anything!*

As we advance, we must remember to focus on the concept of gratitude. Nothing will keep us advancing forward with more joy than possessing a thankful heart. To live the word *gratitude*, we must make the conscious choice to focus on the good in our lives each day. If we want more of anything in life, the quickest way to get there is to appreciate what we already have. The majority of us live focusing on what we don't have, what others have, and how we never have enough. How can our lives be happy or successful when we live with an ungrateful heart? They cannot. We must live the word *grateful* in every way we can. When we catch ourselves being ungrateful, we must get ahold of our thoughts, especially when things aren't going our way, and find the treasures to appreciate in our life. If we can come up with one thing to be grateful for, I guarantee we can come up with two, three, and even more.

Gratitude helps us live with composure. What does the word *composure* bring up? How can we live this word to help our advancement? Our journey to success will undoubtedly bring great increase and significant hardship. We get to decide how we will deal with both. When we are graced with great increase, composure looks like humility and gratitude. When we experience hardship or challenge, composure looks like steadiness under strain. When we're composed, we hold an evenness of mind and emotion. Composure carries itself as tall and elegant regardless of what is changing outside of us. Walk, talk, eat, move, and speak with composure. Live the essence of this word each day and great change will occur.

To make sure we advance just a little, each and every day, it is helpful to replace resolutions with *living words*. Words are concepts. Concepts when practiced become habits, and habits become deeply embedded virtues. Whatever word or words we choose, we must be visionary in how we can apply these words as verbs to all areas of our lives—from how we speak, eat, move, take care of ourselves, communicate, walk, dress, work, and so on.

Coachable Moment

You're five foot nothin'. A hundred and nothin'. And you have barely a speck of athletic ability. And you hung in there with the best college football players in the land for two years. You're gonna walk outta here with a degree from the University of Notre Dame. In this life, you don't have to prove nothin' to nobody but yourself. Am I making myself clear?
— *The custodian in* Rudy, *the movie*

I know that the changes you see from living words will be immeasurable, and the happiness and success you experience will be more stable. When you practice something enough, it becomes part of you—a part of your character. There is nothing more appealing to others than a person of good character. Such people are focused. Focus requires that you be mentally tough. Living words will create the mental toughness and resilience necessary to help you develop the maturity to push through when you think you can't do anymore. As you become mentally focused, you will develop the grit to never give up. You will also develop the rest of your inner power.

You have the mental faculties to stay empowered. It's all in your mind-set. You must direct your thoughts to be positively directed, molding your beliefs around the idea that you can achieve anything you set out to achieve. This helps you upgrade.

Flexibility
Focus + FLEXIBILITY = Advancement

Life is forever surprising for all of us. Life lessons, both good and bad, are experienced throughout our journey toward increased success and fulfillment. None of us is exempt from life's sharper edges. The more rigid we are—the more we resist change, challenge, and failure—the more we draw those negatives into our lives. We cannot succeed without flexibility. We must all learn to roll with life.

You are here to evolve. The signature purpose and intention behind life's sharper edges is to provide you that very opportunity. Without trials, there can be no advancement. What might seem like an enemy will likely turn out to be the only possible thing that could have caused you enough discomfort to finally move you in another direction. When you move, you are forced to look inside yourself and examine your vulnerabilities. Looking within helps you repurpose. *Repurpose* means that we refine who we are through self-improvement. It requires quite a bit of humility to be flexible, but it is our willingness to humble ourselves that builds our character.

To be flexible, we must embrace change. We must count on life to bring the unexpected and drop it on our doorstep without warning and without our consent. We must be willing to flex and bend in the face of the unexpected. We must not see the unexpected as our enemy. Resistance creates chaos, and chaos only creates more problems. We cannot confuse the concepts of focus or commitment with rigidity or closed-mindedness. When we face the unexpected, we must maintain our focus and be willing to see alternate paths for our advancement. This way we remain open and curious to the potential of all new possibilities rather than staying fearfully focused and holding on to what we know, think, believe, and don't want to change.

Change and uncertainty come into our lives to change us, to energize us, and to bring out our *inner competitor*. Change gets us in touch with our ability to be unstoppable in our pursuit. The more relentless we are, the clearer our purpose becomes. Most of us have a select group of poor work habits we need to improve in order to reach the new levels of success we desire. When change and uncertainty visit, we tend to figure out more quickly where we are in need of the most improvement. Here is a great truth: *Whenever we're standing in the weaker position, the improvements we need to make become brilliantly magnified.* This is a gift.

We must be willing to pivot on a dime, shift what we're doing, and explore new options whenever we're called to do so.

Is a lack of predictability uncomfortable? Yes, sometimes horribly so. We have the choice in any moment to run from what is uncomfortable or learn from it. If we choose to learn from it, we give ourselves the opportunity to work through it. Think of a palm tree. When a storm comes, the palm tree appears weak to the winds and pressures as it bends all the way over. However, the more a palm tree bends, the stronger it becomes from within. This is the true value of flexibility for us as well. The more we can bend to change, the stronger we become. Most often in life we're bent, not broken.

Coachable Moment

In real life, being relentless is a state of mind that gives you the strength to achieve, to survive, to overcome, to be strong when others are not. It means craving the end result so intensely that the work becomes irrelevant.

—*Tim S. Grover*

To deal with uncertainty, we have to move with it. One of my favorite books is called *Stand Like Mountain, Flow Like Water*, by Brian Luke Seaward, PhD. The book's title and theme reinforces the truth that business, life, and love are fluid; therefore, it is wise to anticipate uncertainty at every turn. We must train ourselves to become adaptable under the pressures of changing circumstances. Flexibility helps us secure existing opportunities, to decrease our stress, and to be open-minded to new opportunities we never could have secured had we been rigid. It is wasteful to struggle with what we cannot control. The unexpected helps us identify the specific areas in which we most need improvement. It helps us accept these weaker points and explore other resources we can use to press forward. For success to blossom, we must consistently reinvent our ideas, thoughts, plans, goals, and, most importantly, ourselves.

Live from a Place of Curiosity

When things change, we feel afraid. That's a normal and healthy response, not one we should condemn ourselves for. In fact, being afraid has some important gifts. Feelings of fear provoke a natural sense of mystery, curiosity, and wonderment for how things are going to work out. When things don't go as planned, we must learn to be curious rather than furious. When things don't go our way, there is a reason.

Got faith? A great acronym from Alcoholics Anonymous for faith is *Fear Ain't In This House*.

Fear blocks our vision, whereas curiosity opens us to new ideas and opportunities.

Curiosity keeps us thirsty for how we can use unexpected changes for our betterment. If we fear being curious and getting outside of our comfort zones, we can only run in place. When we're curious, we crave to know more, to do more, and to set ourselves up to get more. Curiosity inspires us to examine the vulnerabilities that keep us stuck and unable to maximize upon. When we approach business with a sense of adventure, there is no situation, however limiting physically or economically, that cannot be filled to the brim with interest, curiosity, and excited anticipation for how it will all work out. Without curiosity, we are limited in how much we can advance. The more curious and open we are, the wider our horizons will become.

I urge you to enjoy the mystery of your journey. Any and all plans for your advancement will naturally bring feelings of insecurity. That's okay. It's normal to feel that a perfect plan is necessary before you're ready to venture into the unfamiliar. Yet, it is this false belief that most often holds you back from starting. Advancement doesn't happen because you've developed the perfect plan. It happens when you have a plan and have combined it with a sense of reckless abandon. You cannot perfectly plan for the unknown. I encourage you to start working your plan and remain open and flexible to what's next. When you feel fear, look at your advancement the same way you would view driving on an unfamiliar road in the dark. As you continue driving, more of the road is revealed a little bit at a time, giving you the direction you need. To see more of the road, you just have to keep driving.

Ambiguity creates doubt and anxiety, but it also creates a fierce sense of creativity and resourcefulness. We are never more innovative than when we believe our survival is at stake. There is no way *around* ambiguity. We must travel *through* it. When things are uncertain, we must invest ourselves in soul-searching, researching, studying, and finding solutions. We must be resourceful through ambiguous times. The more resourceful we are, the more pioneering we become. Success comes when we have enough self-control to place our desperate and immediate needs on hold, allowing us time to think more logically and clearly about how to gather the resources we need to take rightful action.

When we are unable to see clearly, another way to be resourceful is to look to our past for comfort. Past history is an intelligent and commendable leader in times of uncertainty. We can look back on other uncertain times we have passed through to examine the resiliency skills we used to help get us through. Then we can make use of those skills in our current predicament.

Keep this in mind: Each time something bad has happened to you, you have survived and likely grown wiser. I encourage you to look back and feel a deep sense of trust in yourself to handle what life has brought you today. Your past missteps didn't define you; they trained you. They trained you for this very moment. It is because you've made mistakes that you will be able to handle your current stressors. Past history has likely taught you that it is best not to force ideas onto an unpredictable situation. Whatever you force will work against you. The greatest power you have is to allow solutions the space they need to manifest on their own.

Coachable Moment

If you try to change it, you will ruin it. Try to hold it, and you will lose it.

—Lao Tzu

We must come to embrace that change is the one and only thing we can depend on. Flexibility allows us to move through our changes with some fluidity. The more flexible we are, the more innovative we become. Change forces us to think in novel ways. Stress is actually necessary. Anytime we feel stress, it is a signal that a rigidly held belief we are holding is being challenged. If we hold tight to our old plans, we miss the opportunities the current changes have in store for us.

Coachable Moment

Let me tell you something you already know. The world ain't all sunshine and rainbows. It's a very mean and nasty place and I don't care how tough you are, it will beat you to your knees and keep you there permanently if you let it. You, me, or nobody is gonna hit as hard as life. But it ain't about how hard ya hit. It's about how hard you can get hit and keep moving forward. How much you can take and keep moving forward. That's how winning is done!

—Sylvester Stallone, Rocky Balboa

Advancement

Focus + Flexibility = ADVANCEMENT

When we add focus to flexibility, we make ourselves resourceful enough to advance. We advance by sticking to our goals with a relentless belief that we can and will overcome obstacles placed at our feet. When we decide to be a person who never quits, we become that person. We move from quitter to go-getter. We start to see the evidence that, as things in our lives change, we grow and progress as a natural byproduct. Progression of any sort is a sign of personal, professional, and emotional advancement. If we take any step, no matter how small, we are advancing.

Moreover, as you take on any endeavor, you will see other people who are trying to accomplish the same thing quit. Each time another pursuer quits, more opportunity opens for you. Staying power is the key to your advancement. As others fall away, your path narrows, placing you among the select few who also made the journey to the top. Then you will find yourself ranked among the elite of the elite because you chose to live the very simple virtue of never giving up. So be the last man—or woman—standing.

The greatest joy to come from succeeding is that the more we advance, the more passionately we fall in love with what we are doing. We experience who we are and the depth of our potential with each tiny step we take toward living our dream. The steps we take grow our wings. We learn to fly. Flying is the freedom we each instinctively crave. The more freedom we have, the more our contentment grows. Further, we become more unselfish as we become more successful and content. When we have worked hard to secure an abundance of resources, we experience less pressure. This gives us the space necessary to help us positively influence and grow our team, to support them in their own success, and to give back to our communities. Success, in its purest form, is more about having the power to give than it is about needing to keep everything we receive.

MARINATE ON THIS

If you fall behind, run faster. Never give up, never surrender, and rise up against the odds.

—*Jesse Jackson*

Part 2
SAFETY NEEDS

The fact is that people are good; give people affection and security, and they will give affection and be secure in their feelings and their behavior.
—Abraham Maslow

For our dreams to flourish and grow, they must have solid ground and healthy soil to sprout from. When we feel our environment is secure (whether corporate or family), it has a positive impact on our productivity and, even more importantly, on our morale. When we feel safe to be who we are, we look forward to coming to work, as do our colleagues, thus reducing absenteeism. Further, feelings of security extend into the emotional well-being both in and outside of the workplace. Love and support at home or work or the lack thereof either greatly increases our sense of ease and productivity or it absolutely destroys it. For this reason, it is crucial that our work environment provide us and our families the appropriate medical benefits, retirement plans, and other things, such as stock options, making us and others feeling more secure about our jobs and the brightness of our future. As an entrepreneur, we must demonstrate that we care for the welfare of ourselves and our colleagues as this creates an atmosphere of trust, which, in turn, encourages loyalty and decreased anxiety. When we feel secure in our work environment, we bring less stress home and vice versa.

Introspection + Emotional Management = Self-Awareness

Your visions will become clear only when you can look into your own heart.
Who looks outside, dreams; who looks inside, awakens.

—C. G. Jung

A great truth to understand is that we are only secure in our lives as we are self-aware. The more we're stretched, the more we advance, the more we have to learn, the more we have to grow; therefore, the more in touch we must consistently be in developing and growing our self-awareness.

There is no greater achievement in life than to *know thy own Self*. What drives each of us as human beings into the deeper questions of life are the challenges, pains, and obstacles we face. Whenever we're being deeply challenged, we are also profoundly inspired, creative, innovative, and steadfast. Or, we at least have that choice. Quitting doesn't teach us anything about what we're capable of. Most people quit out of frustration. To make it to the top, though, we must allow our frustrations to teach us, to grow us, and to make us that much more determined and tolerant.

Sadly, today's tolerance has morphed into celebrating whatever we believe to be true and right, regardless of what others think or feel. This type of tolerance actually becomes divisive, the exact opposite of what authentic tolerance really is. What I mean by tolerance is the old model of tolerance where we each possess the humility to accept other people and their differences from us with the commitment to remain tactful and respectful of them, even when we disagree. This also means that when we voice our disagreement with others that we expect them to respect us in return. We are each entitled to have our own unique views and to be accepted for them rather than rejected with a "you're either for me or against me" attitude.

I believe that it's okay for you to feel frustrated on your path. In fact, I think frustration is essential for who you can become and where you want to go. It is designed to help you break through any narrowing of your focus. This is what it means to be outside of your comfort zone.

A corollary of this is to learn to tolerate your frustration. Try not to let your frustration create division between you and your own goals by allowing it to drive you to quit. Learn to trust yourself and to be a person you can count on when you're on the brink of wanting to give up. You can do this, and you need to do this. We are all underdogs. The greatest victory is always when the underdog wins. So get up and get going! The more you advance, the more you grow, and the more self-aware you become. When things get hard, you must compete. So move ahead knowing that you've got this handled.

INTROSPECTION

INTROSPECTION + Emotional Management = Self-Awareness

To be elite in any area of your life, you must consistently analyze and measure your thoughts and emotions. This type of self-examination empowers you to rely exclusively on the observation of your own mental state to succeed in your life, in love, in your career, and in your relationships.

Ignorance is *not* bliss. It is your self-awareness that gifts you with the pristine ability to manage your more harmful emotions. The ignorant spray their toxicity all over their environment with a sense of entitlement, infecting everyone and everything around them. They do not turn within; they turn to shame and blame. Let's not do this.

Your purpose here on earth is to evolve. You must be able to turn to yourself whenever necessary for the insight you need. The depth of your self-awareness is directly correlated to the type of happiness that has longevity attached to it. Life without happiness is not a well-lived life at all. Being self-aware helps you in every area of your life, especially in your relationships. What are all successful lives and businesses really about at their foundation? Good relationships.

To be introspective means to look inside ourselves. It is the way we get to know our own thoughts and emotions. It is imperative to know ourselves well, to have healthy relationships, and to truly love who we are. The goal is to be a person that we, ourselves, can love, like, count on, trust, and respect. We all need more self-love. We must believe in the value of empowering ourselves and in empowering and promoting others. We need to trust there is no such thing as "not enough" in this life. When this belief is truly ingrained, it allows us to go inside and find all the wealth, happiness, and abundance that exist in our own heart.

Your liking and respecting yourself is the foundation of health upon which all of life is built. Healthy people introspect. It allows you to analyze yourself and identify what and where your trigger points are. These trigger points teach you when to act on an emotion, and when it may be smarter to stay quiet.

Leading a successful life and running a successful business is a matrix of balancing conflict and progress. It is impossible to lead yourself effectively without being able to first identify the emotions that drive you. If you do not know your own emotions, you cannot effectively manage them. Empathy and understanding give you the guidance on how to effectively lead yourself and then others. Therefore, the first person to get to know and manage is *yourself*.

Here's a fascinating fact: Healthy people come to therapy. They come to therapy to learn how to deal with the unhealthy people in their lives who drive them crazy. Unhealthy people, however, find zero value in introspection, and this is exactly why they drive others crazy and lose one relationship after another. When you're equipped with self-awareness, you become alert more quickly to the negative relationships holding you back. Negativity in relationships often doesn't change. For example, if you're in a relationship with someone who is never happy and highly critical, he or she is not likely to change simply because you and probably others have brought it to their attention. However, this does not mean you cannot make the necessary changes in yourself to maintain your boundaries. You can make sure to have as little interaction with such people as possible or choose to end these relationships all together. If this person is your boss or on your team, you must learn to focus on yourself, your work, your goals, and your objectives, and only interact with him or her when absolutely necessary. When interacting, keep the topic focused on facts and away from the negative emotions this person may be trying to provoke in you. Facts and other measurable information are lifesavers when interacting with difficult people.

Introspection is one of the most underutilized tools in the success box. Reflecting on and gaining insight into our deeper beliefs about life, success, and people are part of a lifelong process. They cannot be accomplished in an isolated moment. It is in our times of self-reflection that we land upon our aha moments. These moments are precious because they help us define who we are and to identify the various ways we are capable of having an influence in this world for the greater good. The more we know about ourselves, the more power we have to positively influence others and make a difference.

Does introspection hurt? It can, but it leads us directly into the places we need to grow.

Over time, introspection gives us a wonderful gift—it enables us to trust our own brilliance.

So how do you accomplish this?

Make the Time

You must make time for introspection.

I encourage you to schedule time for self-reflection into your daily routine. This is time for you and you only.

How do you get to know other people? You spend quality time with them. Do the same for yourself with yourself. The more deeply you understand who you are, the more power you have in creating and influencing positive change in your life and in establishing the healthy and secure dynamics in your relationships that you crave.

During this self-reflection time, ask yourself what your core beliefs are about yourself and other people. Here are some other good avenues to pursue during this time:

- Ask, *How do I need to grow to keep advancing?*
- Allow your thoughts to wonder as you reflect on past leadership experiences, your role with people, how your thoughts, attitudes, beliefs, conversations, conflicts, challenges, and feelings had an impact on you and those around you. How did your beliefs help or harm these situations?
- What aspects of yourself do you see as strengths and what areas do you see that could use some growth?

What you believe about people ultimately determines how you treat them.

What you feel about yourself directly impacts the way you allow others to treat you.

When you carve out time for self-reflection, view it as having a heart-to-heart conversation with yourself.

Let go of your to-do list for a few minutes, shut off the phone, and take a deep breath. Breathing and self-reflection are medicine for your soul. Do a lot of both.

Builds Beliefs

Introspection helps to discipline our focus, especially when we engage in the process of writing down our thoughts and reflections. Writing aligns us with the deeper levels of self-understanding we crave.

If our beliefs about us or others are negative, we must work to shift these thoughts to the positive. We must adopt the belief that people want to do a good job and that they desire challenging work and new opportunities to enhance their personal growth. When we project the belief that people want to hear what we have to say and that they deeply desire to produce incredible results, this is the environment we will actually create. Our attitude is powerful enough to bring people down or uplift them. People work harder and smarter when supported by someone who believes in them.

What we focus on is what we will experience, whether our beliefs are true or not. If we have hard-working, inspired people in our lives yet hold the view that people are lazy and unproductive, it will be nearly impossible for us to see people for who they really are. Security cannot be developed when we focus on what people are not enough of for us. The more we self-reflect, see, and grow the positive in ourselves, the more we will project this belief and focus onto other people.

What do your actions and reactions tell other people about you? Think about how you lead your life and lead others and what you'd like to change. Capture those aha moments gained from examining yourself, and use them to strengthen your relationships.

Introspection is a form of taking action. It is your personal investment in yourself. It supplies you with the all-important character trait of being emotionally intelligent. If you do not reflect on where you have been—what has and has not worked in the past—you put yourself at risk of destroying your dreams for the future.

Allows You to Live Wholeheartedly

Introspection brings us into a solid, reality-based, authentic relationship with ourselves. When we live authentically, we free ourselves from living the image we assume others want us to be. We become fearless. We begin living from the self-determination of what it means to be *who we are.* This is true freedom. This is our God-given right and what we deeply want to experience. When we know ourselves intimately, we become more resolute in our abilities and humble in knowing we aren't perfect. This knowing helps us to bond and secure healthier and more loving attachments to others. We no longer strive to be the flawless version of some fictitious model human being. Instead, we strive to enhance the person we already are, faults and all. We develop self-compassion, which turns to empathy, and this empathy is what softens our beliefs and judgments of others.

When we live wholeheartedly, it brings our life into a genuine and relaxed flow. We no longer merely *survive* life—we *live* it. When we self-reflect, we uncover the powers that lay quietly beneath our fears and insecurities.

Most of us live our lives overcompensating for our perceived weaknesses as a way to deny their impact on our life. For example, I used to be a pleaser. I grew up feeling very insecure about myself and my likability. I used pleasing as a way to get others to like and accept me. Thankfully, I grew out of this response. I realize my people-pleasing may have kept me out of the line of fire at some points during my upbringing, but it destroyed me as an adult because I was consistently living my life based on someone else's needs or idea of me. I was taken advantage of more often than I would like to admit. It wasn't until I began feeling deeply lonely because I felt that no one really knew me that I began to change. It took courage to start being the authentic version of me, and I lost some relationships as a result, but this also completely set my life straight. Being taken advantage of now almost never happens. This feels much better than pleasing. Overcompensating has a negative impact because it is inauthentic. It involves pretending to be something or someone we are not. Unacknowledged insecurities create resentment rather than joy. We cannot advance our vision if we're failing to enjoy the journey. In overcompensating for our perceived faults, we are likely to hit burnout more quickly, become more anxious, and find our lives and careers more taxing.

In reality, there are some positive benefits to glean from our fears. Fear is the one emotion powerful enough to provoke us into self-reflection because we will do nearly anything to stop feeling fear. Understanding our fears is the way to conquer them.

I have come to understand, through my own self-reflection, that underneath every fear I have felt is a hidden power. The powers underneath my fears essentially lead me into feeling more safe and secure in my life. I realize this is counterintuitive, but it is nonetheless true. Let's examine what some of these powers are.

Knowledge
Knowledge is the strength underneath our fear of not having confidence.

Knowledge is power. It is difficult to feel safe or secure when we lack the knowledge necessary to make us versatile and flexible in our daily challenges. Without knowledge, we function from a weaker position, especially in the throes of conflict or negotiation. The weaker our position, the more fear we experience. Preparation and knowledge, on the other hand, naturally endow us with more confidence. If we lack the information we need, we should humble ourselves to verbalize, "I don't know," and then seek to find out the knowledge we are missing. We must always be willing to go back to the drawing board and fill in the missing pieces in order to avoid being in the weaker position going forward.

Openness

Openness is the strength below our fear of change.

Having knowledge is essential for us to succeed, but we must not allow ourselves to become so fixed or rigid in our thinking that we come to view our knowledge as the *only* correct knowledge. When we think what we know is sufficient, we close our minds to new information and learning that could greatly benefit us. Being open is a strength that makes us more likeable and approachable. When we are open, others perceive us as easier to work with. Rigid thinking, and its subsequent limitations, is the way we typically overcompensate for our fear of change. We falsely believe that if we know enough, we are somehow impermeable. However, closed-mindedness and rigid rules do not help us, especially not in our relationships with others. No one likes overcontrolling, micromanaging people. We need to keep our minds open to new ideas, to correction, and to broadening and deepening our knowledge base and skill set. When we open our minds in such ways, the world opens to us.

Patience

Patience is the strength beneath our fear of the unknown.

Impatience is a reaction to living in the grey area of uncertain results. To overcompensate for this fear, we tend to become reactive, which puts us at risk to make less than stellar decisions. Impulsive decisions, in most cases, push our desired results even further away.

In practicing patience, we develop the strength and grace to allow things to take their natural course. Being patient makes us smarter. We come to realize that there are some solutions worth waiting for. When we give ourselves a little time and space, we can see past our reactive emotions to forecast more effective solutions and more realistic outcomes.

Boldness

Boldness is the strength beneath our fear of conflict.

Many of us cower under conflict. That's a natural reaction. No one likes feeling attacked. When under siege, we hear our instincts telling us what to do and say while feeling overwhelmed with the projected negative consequences our acting boldly could bring. All of this hinders us from stepping up to the plate to try to get a hit.

However, it is possible to be bold and fair and trust that the consequences of our actions will only help propel our success forward. Boldness takes practice. It is a skill to practice and hone. But the more we stand up to life's conflicts, the more trust we will develop in ourselves to take care of ourselves.

Here's a fact to ponder and act on: Unless we say what we want, we won't get what we want. And this requires boldness.

Allowing

Allowing is the strength beneath the fear of not having control.

Often we're so fear-based that we overcorrect by being controlling. We can become so afraid that things aren't going to go our way that we start forcing things into place. We become so focused on coercing that we dismiss the negative impacts this behavior is having on others and on the result we are aiming for. It is not at all enjoyable to spend time around or work with controlling, high-strung, bossy people. These types of people suck the joy, cooperation, and collaboration out of every experience. We cannot effectively operate this way.

It is vital we learn to allow people to be who they are, to allow situations to be what they are, and to allow ourselves to be who we are without self-recrimination. Allowing is a tremendous power because it keeps the flow of things open and our resistance to change at bay. It is amazing what develops when we allow things to manifest in their own way and own timing. When we allow the process of success to have its own life, succeeding is much easier.

Courage

Courage is the strength below our fear of failure.

Whenever we feel paralyzed with fear, courage is about the last thing we feel. Fear has two waves. The first is shock. When we're in shock, courage cannot come. Luckily, shock is a short-lived emotional state. Once shock passes, our mind begins to unscramble, allowing us to think with more clarity, which is the second wave. We start to see a path to our solution and are better able to approach our problem with an adrenalized, yet focused, readiness. This is the birth of courage.

Many people assume that courage is natural for some of us but not for others. This may be true, but it's not the end of the matter. Most of us have to talk ourselves into courage. Think back to when you were a very young child and jumping off the high dive for the first time. There was a lot of self-talk going on inside of you before you jumped. This self-talk process holds true for every novel step we take in life, no matter our age. All of us can cultivate courage. Thinkers as far back as Plato and Aristotle realized this and taught it. This is because courage is not something we *have* but something we *do*. And since it is an action, we can all learn to perform it.

Many people perform best when they are under pressure. Fear pressures us to yield rather than move forward. We can overcome fear by responding to it with courage—that is, by acting courageously. Courage exceeds fear and overcomes it. As the actor John Wayne once said, "Courage is being scared to death—but saddling up anyway." So take the leap and practice courage. It won't let you down.

Quiet

Quiet is the power beneath our fear of not being good enough.

When we feel nervous, the natural tendency is to talk too much. Nervous talking is not success-driven communication, and in reality, the more we talk, the more insecure we get, and unfortunately, the more we keep talking.

In a social world dominated by extroversion, the strength of being quiet is one many people never utilize or study. But when we are quiet, we present ourselves as attentive and calm. People want and need to be heard and understood, so when facing insecurities of not being good enough, we must learn to listen. When people feel heard, they become interested in the listener, and in this way we invite the conversation toward ourselves, which in turn gives us more confidence. Feelings of security don't need to be backed with self-promotion or convincing. Instead, they come through our ability to be calm, measured, and quiet.

Mindfulness

Mindfulness is the strength below our feeling of panic.

Fear is a power all unto itself. This is because fear is a fuel. Whenever we're fearful, we jump into action as a way to remove the fear as quickly as possible. Fear causes problems because it makes us too mercurial. When we are this way, we become emotional and incredibly unpredictable in our mood and actions. Out of fear or panic, we jump into action without putting much thought behind what we're doing. We see this type of impulsivity in athletes during key moments of a game. How often have we seen an athlete choke and jump the line before the play has been called, or jump out of or off the starting blocks before the whistle has blown for the race? How many poor decisions have been made in business meetings out of the pressure and impulsivity to find an immediate solution to a game-changing obstacle?

We can respond to fear differently and even beneficially. We can make it our greatest asset if we use it to practice a state of heightened mindfulness. When in a state of emergency, fear makes us acutely aware of what is going on. If we can stay calm, we can have increased clarity on the frontlines of our own critical decisions. This is what US Airlines pilot Captain "Sully" Sullenberger did when his aircraft with 155 people onboard was struck by a large flock of geese during liftoff from New York's LaGuardia Airport. Both of the plane's engines were so damaged that they no longer provided any thrust. Captain Sully had two options: either return to LaGuardia or land at an airport near New Jersey. He quickly determined that his plane was in no condition to survive either option, so he decided to land his plane in the nearby Hudson River. His skill and decision-making that day saved all 155 people onboard. He used a fearful situation to focus his mind and ended up saving lives, including his own. On top of this, Sully later had to remain mindful as the FAA was doing all they could to prove his decision-making that day was reckless and shortsighted. He remained patient, calm, and confident in his knowledge and experience, not veering from what he knew the truth to be. This allowed him to keep hold of himself under the pressure of the interrogation. Others with a different temperament may have fractured under the pressure and been unable to articulate what happened on that fateful day. But Sully remained clear, courageous, and undaunted.

The more we advance, the more insecurity we are sure to face. At the same time that we are facing fears and advancing, we also develop the security and confidence we've always desired to have. The more we develop ourselves, the more we learn to lead from our strengths rather than our fears. This helps us view the world as not such a scary place. We start to move with a certain polish through our troubles. We may be impacted by our troubles, but we do not have to be flattened by them.

To lead from our strengths, we must use our trials as tests of our character and practice living from the power beneath our fears. We must choose to rise to the occasion and go against our biological programming to naturally regress under stress. Attaining this type of composure takes practice and awareness, but if we're going to practice anything, why not let it be leading from our strengths?

———

I tell my patients that all types of self-reflection help them live more enthusiastically and valiantly. All the answers you need can be found by going within. If you want to know who you are and how you work, you must look into the cracks and crevices of your insecurities and ask yourself honest questions about your views on life, people, love, business, finances, responsibilities, and leadership. Self-reflection gives you answers and the opportunity to live what you learn.

As you discover what makes you tick, you discover your strengths and weaknesses. Knowing where you thrive and where you lack is incredible knowledge. These are the aha moments that come from self-reflection. These moments of insight are your "God-shots" of innovation. The ideas you're struggling to find will be there if you persist in looking for them.

If you live only through your mind and don't make time to self-reflect, you live largely through control, which causes you to fight life rather than flow with it by learning to ride the waves. It's so much better to learn to ride life's waves. It is more exalting and growth-promoting to live life this way than by exhausting yourself trying to battle or outrun life's breakers. Always remember, each wave you're on, no matter how big or intimidating, will eventually pass and become calm again. So take this view: A difficult problem is a master teacher. Learn from it and grow wise beyond your years.

Coachable Moment

You gain strength, courage, and confidence by every experience in which you really stop to look fear in the face. You are able to say to yourself, 'I lived through this horror. I can take the next thing that comes along.'

—*Eleanor Roosevelt*

Emotional Management

Introspection + EMOTIONAL MANAGEMENT = Self-Awareness

To harness our emotions, we must first do some work to feel and understand them. As we study how we feel, we will find that emotions follow a simple pattern of rising and falling. We struggle the most with any emotion when we're at the peak of its wave. There we find ourselves disconnected from our rational thinking mind, which means we cannot make sound decisions. Impulsive decisions are always and in all ways emotional decisions that we often live to regret. What we want to try and cultivate is having Presence of Mind while in the midst of riding the waves of life, just as Sully did when landing his plane in the Hudson River.

I love the idea of having Presence of Mind, but it is *not* easy to achieve. It is a transient state of mind and something we practice again and again until it becomes a more consistent and stable part of our character. Eckhart Tolle says, "When you take your attention into the present moment, a certain alertness arises. You become more conscious of what's around you, but also, strangely, a sense of presence that is both within and without." If you are in the moment and present to what is happening within you and outside of you, you cannot lose. Take time to be settled before you respond or make any decisions. You deserve this. Never let life, relationships, or business bully you. Life can wait until you have the right answers. It is better to take your time to make the right decision than it is to deal with the cleanup after having made the wrong one.

For most of us, our emotions are in control with our thoughts a good ten steps behind. When we have Presence of Mind, we are better able to manage the emotional waves we're on, no matter how steep and scary they may be. Instead of being ten steps behind our emotions, we are more in the moment where rational thought and action have an opportunity to combine. Travis Bradberry, the author of *Emotional Intelligence 2.0* and a fellow writer for *Entrepreneur*, explains why emotions are so challenging: "Since our brains are hardwired to make us emotional creatures, your first reaction to an event is always going to be an emotional one. You have no control over this part of the process. You do control the thoughts that follow that emotion, and you have a great deal of say in how you react to an emotion—as long as you are aware of it."

Here's the way I like to express this situation. Emotions, good and bad, are no more mature than a two- to five-year-old. What do two- to five-year-olds need? Your time, love, and attention. If you give your emotions a moment's attention, they tend to settle down and make sense. Ignoring negative emotions builds anger and resentment, increasing the likelihood of a future explosion. Likewise, ignoring excitement or joy increases our chances of entering prematurely into agreements or other celebratory behaviors, which can create issues we later regret. We must slow down enough to think about what we're feeling. When you expose your emotions with little regard or forethought in how they may have an impact, you end up creating unwanted drama or unnecessary messes and conflicts that you will need to cleanup. So, to be successful, you not only need to learn to control the waves of the emotional rollercoaster but also how fast it goes. This takes practice.

Here are some approaches I suggest you learn and practice on your way to emotional self-management.

Know When to Do Nothing

When we are upset, frustrated, or angry, it is in our best interest to stay silent until we achieve some level of self-mastery. At the onset of any strong emotion, we may feel venting will make us feel better, but in most cases it never does. We end up regretting things we have said and done. This is especially true in our relationships, whether they are personal or business. In life, results come and go, but feelings are forever. If we publicly criticize others, it may seem as if they eventually get over it, but inside they never do.

Impeccable self-management skills are necessary to be a successful human being. Living in a world that has largely become self-centered, mean, egotistical, smug, entitled, and greedy, we need more people who live on the side of caring deeply about the well-being, happiness, and success of others. Keep in mind: the most secure person is not the person who is always right; rather, it is the person who is wise enough to know when to keep the peace.

When we lack self-regulation skills, our emotions become turbulent success-killers. This is not what we want.

Lack of self-regulation most commonly presents as a lack of patience. Patience is slow because it involves waiting, but for most of us the prospect of achieving success feels like an emergency because it's something we all want right now! What we need, however, is not to rush after success. Success comes more fully and naturally when we slow down our emotional pace to become more intentional, more methodical, and more meticulous in our pursuit. Rushing doesn't require any emotional management, but patience and diligence do. We cannot rush our way into succeeding, but we can certainly pace our way there.

As an entrepreneur myself, I know that you can have the greatest ideas in the world, but without patience and staying power, you are not likely to see them become actual no matter how genius they may be. To be successful, you must practice patience. Patience is like a muscle: the more you use it, the stronger this virtue becomes.

The negative side effect of impatience is the desire to give in to your doubts and frustrations, which far too often trick you into giving up too easily. In contrast, lasting and sustainable success is not a game of instant gratification. True success is a dynamic, unfolding process built upon change, challenge, hard work, and growth. Patience gives you the determination to stick to a goal despite the odds. It helps cultivate persistence, acceptance, as well as feelings of safety and hope. It allows you to see the big and small pictures, giving you a sense of control over your mind and impulses when things look bleak. When you are patient, you greatly increase your odds of making your personal dreams come true.

Success in and of itself is an art and a discipline, not just a sought-after ideal. For this reason, many people chase an ideal without the necessary skills to get there. A big dream and a great idea don't become successful simply because they exist. Without being able to discipline our thoughts, manage and organize our time, control our emotions, be completely committed to our cause, and have the patience to get through our challenges, thereby further fueling our hope, we are largely handicapped in trying to reach our desired outcomes. It is too easy to get trapped in negative thinking and aggravation. In reality, it is the things we have the strongest feelings for that we focus on. Each of us has the power to generate a state of absolute joy by thinking of all the great things that have happened in our lives, just as we can cause a relatively instant state of depression by focusing on what we believe we lack. To be happy and successful, we have to set our thoughts on what makes us successful and happy.

Focus on your dreams, and walk through the world as if you have already achieved them. Focus strictly on what you want and take nothing for granted. As you focus on the good, you will begin to manifest those thoughts. And actions follow thoughts. This is why writing my goals has become a key ingredient to my success and that of many others. My goals reflect my thoughts and desires. Writing them down infuses me with an attitude of hope and success. I trust that if I can think these goals up that they are a real possibility for my life. The moment I put well-defined action behind my goals, I begin to achieve what I have set out to achieve. Putting my goals onto my vision board makes my goals visual to me. Seeing them in front of me makes me keenly aware of what I am reaching for and why reaching for them is so important to me. My goals are the map of my life that give it the depth and meaning I desire to experience. I also have many goals written down that aren't ready to launch yet. These are the goals I know not to activate right now. It is important to know when not to move on a goal as we may need to wait for timing and opportunity to partner up before we can succeed in a certain area.

Better Yourself

The goal of emotional management is to better ourselves and to guarantee we can show up in life with the ability to, at the very least, control our own emotional state.

We are never more acutely aware of the pressures of the moment than when facing fear and uncertainty. Our survival instincts force us to pay attention to every nuance of our uncertain situation. When in fight-or-flight mode, we become connected to everything we see, listen to, read, learn, try, and practice in order to make our situation solvable. This emotional awareness helps us to trust ourselves. In trusting ourselves, we discover new pathways to success.

Challenges teach us that we can do better. They bring depth of character. We learn to pull from an inner strength we didn't know we had. We become remarkable, resourceful, and confident in our abilities to be successful in life, no matter what we face. We become a person of mindful action. And we develop a strong will—one that is fundamental to our success and continual advancement.

To create great success, you need something to struggle against and struggle for. The aim in life should not be to avoid challenges or stressful situations or emotions but to have the right ones. You should not avoid worry but learn to care about the right things. You should not strive to be without fear but confront the right fears with strength and passion. What you become is a direct result of what you are willing to learn and endure.

I believe that all success starts as an attitude. I make it a practice to live the way I would be living if I felt totally successful and secure. I take on every imaginative way I can ponder to live with the most productive mind-set. The first place I start is with my posture. I ask myself, *What is the posture of undefeated success?* I see it as someone who stands tall, and in their tallness, others sense their depth and conviction as gained through their trials and errors. If you want to be more patient and trust in your success, then stand tall and put a smile on your face. Walk with a purpose. Your brain will believe you and adjust your mood and thinking around the stance of your posture. Your thoughts will believe what you are feeling as you stand taller, helping you to more effortlessly increase your success. If you believe it, you will become it. And as you become it, you will get to live the experience of it. All of your systems—body, mind, and spirit—are intimately connected. Take advantage of using all of them to your benefit.

Success is truly the grind of mind over matter. To develop more self-control, we must read, live, process, and utilize our emotions. The more mindful we are of what we are feeling, the more in touch we are with the pros and cons of acting out those emotions.

When we are all over the place emotionally, we cannot trust our own responses and neither can anyone else trust us. This turns nearly everything into a potential, impulsive disaster. *So learn to slow down the urge to be right.* We must take the necessary time to taste our words before spitting them out. We must ask ourselves what is more important—being right or becoming successful?

Self-Awareness

Introspection + Emotional Management = SELF-AWARENESS

When we combine introspection with emotional management, we develop our self-awareness.

When we are self-aware, we have a clear perception of who we are, including our strengths, weaknesses, thoughts, values, beliefs, motivations, and emotions. When we acknowledge these qualities in ourselves, we better accept and embrace these same qualities in others.

To succeed at the highest levels, we must be addicted to self-improvement. The more we advance our dreams and visions, the more fitness and growth will be required of us.

Being self-aware sets us up for success because it gives us the feelings of safety and security we need to establish the bonds necessary to build our empire. It helps us understand ourselves, other people, and how they perceive us. It brings insight into acknowledging our own emotions and our responses to them in the moment.

Finally, self-awareness is our greatest skill when it comes to negotiating and sustaining important relationships. The more self-aware I have become, the happier and the more secure I feel within myself and within the structure of my life. Developing my self-awareness has made me more resilient, hopeful, understanding, tolerant, intuitive, and less fearful of other people and the world at large. Self-awareness creates the roots that delve deeply in the earth of my own psyche. It provides me with a mindfulness of my emotional process that I can depend on. This helps me open my heart and my mind to new people, things, and opportunities and to know with more clarity if those new people, things, and opportunities are right for me. Self-awareness has put me deeply in touch with my own sense of right and wrong and continues to be the greatest gift I give myself. If anyone is going to know and love me on all levels, it must first be me.

The development of your self-awareness is the most important step you can take in creating the life you want. It allows you to become the master of your internal world, which will protect you from acting out your more impulsive and potentially destructive impulses. Wherever you have mastery over yourself, you can accomplish anything and everything under the sun.

Where you focus your attention, emotions, reactions, and behaviors determines where you will go in life and how far. Having self-awareness gives you great understanding into overseeing where your thoughts and emotions are taking you. It also allows you to have the forethought and flexibility to change direction whenever necessary.

Until you are aware of your thoughts, emotions, words, and behaviors in the moment they are occurring, you will struggle. The greatest gift you offer to this world is to know yourself, your reactions, and what drives you.

MARINATE ON THIS

People need to know that they have all the tools within themselves. Self-awareness, which means awareness of their body, awareness of their mental space, awareness of their relationships - not only with each other, but with life and the ecosystem.

—Deepak Chopra

Belief + Action = Fearlessness

Why, having been endowed with courageous
heart of a lion, do we live as mice?
—**Brendan Bouchard**

As we travel along the equation-ladder of success and advance our dream, we are continually developing and growing into more capable human beings who are developing the potential to lead others. We are also engaging in the process of learning to hold firm to our dreams and to value the *art* of being emotionally disciplined. The more complete we become, the more developed, and the more self-aware, the more we live filled with curiosity, hope, and confidence. The more secure we feel, the more confidence we have to live fearlessly.

What does it mean to be fearless? It means we make the brave choice to live our lives completely stripped down and authentic to who we are. To be fearless, we must dare to be different. We must lead from our heart and be heroic enough to break from the establishment. We must stop hiding behind a façade of what we think others assume we should be doing and allow ourselves to be exposed as who we really are. When we show our *true selves* to the world, we put ourselves at risk to be ridiculed and rejected, and we ignite the projection of jealousy others may have toward us.

Does this sound risky?

Of course it is.

But the benefits are amazing. The more fearless we are, the more genuine we become. In being true to ourselves, we give ourselves the highest opportunity to be successful. There is no dream worth achieving if it doesn't set us apart, in some way, from others.

So let's move onto our next success equation. It will help us cultivate our fearlessness.

Belief

BELIEF + Action = Fearlessness

Everything we do in life should be done with the intention of evolving the belief we have in ourselves. Each step we take is an opportunity to show ourselves that we're capable of going even further. Each new step teaches us something new about ourselves. Our successes and our failures educate us and make us more self-aware.

The equations we've discussed thus far have been designed to help us become fit and fearless so we can push ourselves out into the world with the confidence to take our dreams to the next level. Like any meaningful journey, we will surely face hardship and challenge that will rock our beliefs to the core. Be ready. Expect them. And know that each time we advance, we will find ourselves in new territory. Each new territory will require courage, thoughtfulness, and exploration. Each new territory forces us to get back to our basics, to start again from the first equation by refining the vision of our dream, once again allowing us to grow from the new place we've been planted.

When I was a competitive figure skater, each new jump or skill I learned forced me to practice and revisit the fundamentals of my already mastered basic skills. Getting back to the basics helped me assimilate the simplicity of what was underneath every new skill or jump I would be learning. All new levels of success bring a sense of accomplishment—but also fear and a lack of knowledge on how to accomplish what is next. As a figure skater, I would start by visualizing the new skill in my mind or watching others perform this skill on video. I then added the actions, knowledge, time, and practice to that vision which were necessary to achieve outwardly what I could see inwardly. All new skills sprout from the basics of what we already know. Therefore, to grow our belief in ourselves, we must revisit the confidence we have developed in our basic knowledge that can help us achieve at the new level of success we have progressed to.

The more experience you have with risk, the more opportunity you have for success. With each risk comes a lesson, and each lesson helps you connect with how much potential you really have. Your potential is truly unlimited. Each new level of success requires a new and improved version of you. There will be fear along this journey each time you advance to a new place. Expect the belief you hold of yourself to be challenged along the way. The good news is this: you each have the potential to grow your belief in yourself to be as vast, as powerful, and as successful as you choose. The only limits that exist are those you self-create and believe in.

On this journey, the only thing you have to do to be fearless is to hit the ball that is in front of you. This is something for you to work on. It comes down to overcoming falsely held ideas in your perceived limits and not giving energy to the fears that feed those limiting beliefs. Fear is going to be a natural part of any success endeavor. Don't fight it. Instead, learn to focus on the right or important things to fear and then break through them.

Believing in ourselves, or really believing in anything, is something that doesn't have an end point because beliefs are continuous. We can believe as deeply and largely in ourselves as we choose. I ask myself all the time what is the real difference between me and someone like Oprah Winfrey? My answer is that her belief in herself is bigger (at this point anyway) than my belief is in myself. I see Oprah as someone to model myself after in terms of how vastly and deeply she believes in herself and what her capabilities are. I don't want her life or her purpose because she does that superbly on her own. There will always and only be one Oprah Winfrey, just as there will always and only be one me. I have the deep desire to have my own impact on this world, and Oprah has been and continues to be a powerful influence to watch and learn from. I don't believe (I could be wrong) that Oprah saw every ounce of her journey laid out perfectly in front of her before she achieved it. I think as her career grew, her life took directions she couldn't have anticipated at the beginning of her journey. I am certain that her directions changed greatly over the course of time as she evolved and had more resources and awareness to create new and different opportunities for herself. Like Oprah, my life and the dreams I see directly laid out in front of me, including the writing of this book, will collide with timing, available resources, changes in direction, and new opportunities as I continue to develop and evolve. I deeply believe that as we expand our beliefs, so do our life opportunities grow. We can only grow our vision as much as we grow ourselves.

Furthermore, we must always keep in mind that failing is another form of succeeding. Each time we fail, we learn the essential pieces of our skill, knowledge, or resources that were missing that we will need to succeed on our next try. In this way our failures contribute greatly to our success. Each time we get back up after a setback, we develop a more secure belief in ourselves and in our capabilities to fight on and succeed. The belief we have in ourselves forms as a direct result of experiencing triumph over our challenges. *If there is a problem, there is a solution.* If we can get through one challenge, we can be sure that we can get through two, three, four, or countless more. To pursue our dreams, we have to be absolutely convinced we can achieve them. When we face a challenge, we get pulled from the familiar. Challenges test our character and our abilities to rally and come out on top. But if we refuse to quit, we cannot ultimately fail.

How badly do you want your vision to become a reality? That's your most important question.

If you truly believe in your vision and yourself, you can make your vision happen. And if fear is holding you back, I advise you to commit to doing the exact things you fear so you won't fear them anymore.

Believing Is Essential to Success

What exactly is believing? Many people hold the misconception that believing simply means wishing. They believe if they wish for something long enough that this is the same as believing in it. Hence, they wish for certain outcomes or dreams to have fulfilling results without taking any form of action. With this approach, all the goodness and success they desire stays stuck in potential. Potential is energy that does not move. Potential is like having a Ferrari sitting in a parking lot with the engine running but the gas pedal never getting pushed. In other words, potential is energy that stays in the invisible and inactive realm of wishing, thinking, and hoping.

Believing is knowing that we are going to succeed, no matter what it takes. We develop this committed perspective by knowing how hard we are willing to work. We must deeply believe that our hard work will eventually lead us to our victory.

When it comes to our success, belief and hard work are essentially everything.

Our beliefs are a direct reflection of the character and mental toughness we have to live our best lives. A negative belief system cannot create success. We make or break our chances at success through the beliefs we hold about our abilities to succeed. Each of us has the ability to create any reality we choose for our lives. Just look at the movie *The Pursuit of Happyness*, starring Will Smith. In this movie, Will's character—Chris Gardner—was literally destitute. He came across a man getting out of a sports car to enter a tall, fancy building, and out of curiosity Chris asked the man what he did for a living and how he could learn to do that same thing. Chris then set about to achieve the impossible by learning how to manage his time impeccably while he worked hard even when he was still homeless and raising a young child. This movie, always and without a doubt, brings me to tears every time I watch it. I've always been the underdog, not in the same sense as Will's character, but the underdog nevertheless. I can relate to fighting what seems like impossible odds and coming out on the other side as having achieved what seemed impossible. This is a beautiful thing. I often wonder if the underdog mentality is essential to success. That if we view succeeding as easy, and we already have the resources, do we really fight as hard for our success and is our success as rewarding? I think not. Achieving what we initially viewed as impossible and having to work hard to gather our own resources are where the juiciness of success is. The juiciness is in overcoming all the odds and coming out victorious.

In this light, I urge you to refuse to set "realistic" goals. Rather, choose to set goals that bring some discomfort with them. Why settle for realistic when you can go for BIG? Our actions follow our thoughts. If we think small, we will live small. When we think big, we will live big.

When we believe in ourselves as wholeheartedly as possible, we make ourselves stand out from those who feel entitled to success coming more easily. We should never hold the idea that success should come easier than it does.

We must fill our headspace with thoughts of success, love, abundance, and prosperity. We must be purposeful in our pursuit. Our headspace is filled with the thoughts we feed it. We are the choosers of our own thinking. Choose well.

Coachable Moment
Rich people believe "I create my life."
Poor people believe "Life happens to me."
—*T. Harv Eker*

How We Think Determines What We Believe

Our thoughts color the way we see all of life and ultimately determine our destiny. To be successful, we have to take a hard look at our ideas about ourselves, money, success, faith, and what we perceive our potential to be. Keep your beliefs hopeful and positive. Negative thinking creates assumed or imaginary roadblocks to success everywhere we turn. If we let negative thinking rule our mind, we are hand-placing roadblocks in front of ourselves. Negative thinking is fixed and unmoving. It works against the flow of forward moving progress. Success takes more than just showing up. We must encourage our innovative thoughts to win by putting positive action behind them. We are going to have bad days, but it is imperative that we know the difference between a bad day and a bad life.

The way you think must be your greatest asset rather than your insurmountable obstacle. Thinking and believing are traits you can practice. Practice makes perfect. If you find yourself thinking negatively or fearfully, catch it, check it, and change it. *Catch* your negative thoughts (acknowledge their presence), *check* them (for truth), and then *change* them (to be proactive). This little slogan is useful in helping you become conscious of your thoughts in order to direct them properly. When you are in control of your thought process, there is no obstacle you cannot bypass.

If you want to be successful, you must eat, drink, sleep, and think thoughts about success. Infuse every thought you have with love, hope, passion, positivity, and trust. When you have fearful and defeatist thoughts, catch them, check them, and change them.

Whatever We Think Is What We Become

Self-belief begins the moment we wake up and open our eyes. It doesn't matter if we have five cents or five million dollars, the process of gaining wealth and obtaining more starts with the right mind-set.

Furthermore, the right mind-set should include the commitment to start taking on challenges to establish a foundation of safety and security that can hold our success. We each have this ability in us. It's not like this potential was doled out to only some of the more fortunate or luckier among us.

Coaching Moment

Amplifying what is great within you will accelerate your life faster than fixing what you think limits you.

—*Brendon Bouchard*

To improve our levels of self-belief, we must refuse to sell ourselves short.

Most of us overestimate others and underestimate ourselves. Why is that? Because when we compare ourselves to others, we see them as smarter, luckier, better, and the like. We must stop these comparisons. We cannot judge someone else's outside by our insides. We must train ourselves to see ourselves as valuable. The value we attach to ourselves will be expressed in all of our actions. How we value ourselves, ultimately, has the largest influence on how others view and treat us. As we are within so we will be without. To be among the elite of the elite, we must feel a deeply felt love and respect for ourselves.

The quickest barometer for knowing how deeply we value ourselves is to examine who and what we attract to ourselves in terms of love, relationship, and opportunity. We cannot change our outside circumstances and expect our insides to fall into place. In other words, a new pair of heels isn't going to make us more successful. A good suit may get us in the door, but it won't walk us up the stairs of success. We need more substance than that. We cannot succeed through entitlement and expectation. We must believe in our purpose so deeply that we attract the types of customers or investors who want to work with us. If we do not believe, to the depth of our core, that we deserve the kind of success we dream of, it is not likely that we will live it. It is that simple and that profound.

Here's something to ponder: When you start completely believing in yourself and your success, you will find the success you're looking for. You will find it because whenever we love anything, we are willing to work as hard as we need for it. You are less likely to give up on anything or anyone you deeply love. This type of commitment will make your path easier because all of the Universe will respond to your desires and the clarity of your intentions. You will attract your success to yourself. If you believe your work has value, others will see the value in your work.

You can absolutely build a successful business.

You can compete with other entrepreneurs.

You can attract the right people to the value of your ideas.

Why? Because of what your ideas offer them.

If you have confidence and hold a firm and deep belief in the impact you can have in this world, you will attract the right people who will believe the same way as you do. When you're engaged with a love affair with your vision and purpose, that love is a beacon of light that will bring you all the right connections to make your dream a reality.

It breaks down to this: Without belief, without love, we would never take action.

Action
Belief + ACTION= Fearlessness

Action is the verb of belief.

Being active researching and testing our beliefs are the ways we bring validity to our ideas. Our actions breathe life, energy, and movement into our beliefs. Our actions are responsible for giving our beliefs form and expression. Our beliefs are only real if we act them out, live them out, and show them to the world. They are the physical expressions of our thoughts, dreams, and desires.

To be remarkable, we must believe in our own power. We must believe, wholeheartedly, that we are the designer and chooser of our own path. We must not wait to be accepted, promoted, selected, or somehow discovered by someone else. In today's technologically advanced world, access is nearly unlimited. We can connect with almost anyone through social media. We can publish our own work, distribute our own music, create our own products, and attract our own funding. We can do almost anything we want, and we don't need to wait for someone else to discover our talents. Let go of waiting for that Oprah moment to happen. Start making it happen. Lead yourself to your Oprah moment in each moment you commit to doing what you love. When that Oprah moment then comes, you can revel in it because it was your own heart, love, blood, sweat, and tears that created it.

On your path to success, it is easy to think you have something intangible, whether it's your ideas, talents, skills, drives, or creativity. I am here to tell you that nothing is intangible. You have what it takes and total access to everything you need to make your dream happen. At every next level, you have to find the courage to push your dream even further out into the world. Listen to your inner voice. That voice is your audience cheering.

If you lack courage, do more research and gain the knowledge you need to push forward with more confidence. Courage is easier to come by when you're well prepared.

There is no entrepreneurial path where every vision is clear, every plan is perfect, or every step is implemented flawlessly. Being a success is never the guaranteed conclusion at the start of anything. Success is a discovery. The more action we take, the more we discover the true potential of our dream. Make time to feel the excitement. Success is never assured. It is earned. If you're willing to work hard and stay determined, who you are as a human being is more than enough. For this reason, don't measure yourself against other people. Pick a goal and measure yourself against that goal.

As we advance to higher and higher levels, more will be demanded of us. Each new level will require something new—some new way in which we will need to stretch and evolve. The more we evolve, the more safety and security we give to our current level of success and all the success we have achieved to this point. At each new level, it is most helpful to list the things we need to move forward from wherever we are. For example, who do we need to model? Who do we need advice from? What information needs to be researched? Who needs to be hired or let go? What networks, systems, or connections do we need to advance from here? Do we need to find investors? A coach? Take out a loan? Grow our business plan? Or do we need to engage in some type of education or training to grow us to that next place? The more action we take in our preparation, the more successfully we will advance.

Preparation must be viewed as if we are training for a boxing match. It's the athlete who believes in her abilities so deeply that she will train long and hard for her fight. When the fight arrives, she has no fear—just the anticipation of the fight. She is filled with excitement because she already knows in her own mind that her opponent has no chance. She enters the ring fearless because she is fully prepared. She is ready to take action. She believes she is destined to win because she's been trained to win, and it is this belief, backed by intense training, that keeps her advancing. The same is true for each of us.

How to Start Preparing for Action

The most powerful place to start when taking action is to put pen to paper. The miracles to come from writing down our goals are unparalleled. Never be without pen and paper on this entrepreneurial journey.

Each new level of our personal and professional actualization will require a new set of goals. As we write out our ideas, we begin the process of creating the next new level and the next. There is no end point to success if we keep dreaming, writing down goals, and taking action on those goals. Writing is kinesthetic, allowing both sides of our brain to work together. Our directions become clear when we write them out, leaning us heavily toward our unlimited potential. The exercise of writing slows us down emotionally and mentally and engages us with the more creative strengths of the right side of our brain. When we are engaged with these strengths, we come up with innovative ideas we likely could not have generated without the task of writing. The strength of the left brain, generated from the task of writing, is an increase in focus and logic. The left-brain activities help us stay on-point and to work through any problems or flaws in the ideas we are generating.

Coachable Moment

The discipline of writing something down is the first step toward making it happen.

—Lee Iacocca

There are no guarantees on any path to success, and this is where having a clear vision and a deep sense of self-awareness help us stay in motion as we move further and further along the road. Deep belief drives us to research, test, question, find answers, develop systems, and accurately predict the results of our movement forward. When we are prepared, we have more confidence. When we feel confident in our knowledge, we are naturally more courageous and willing to take the necessary risks. Risk must always be faced with courage. Because the unknown is always looming, risk is a sure way to discover if we're heading in the right direction. If we are afraid to risk, we put limits on our success because we do not prepare as deeply for our goals as we would if we were risking something. Without risk, we are actively choosing to stay where we are comfortable. I am all for comfort, but we cannot get what we want if we do not risk facing the rejection of going after our desires.

When we fail, we learn very quickly that we took a direction that didn't work. This experience is actually good news. It helps us do what it takes to get readjusted so we can keep going.

Coachable Moment

To move to any new level in your life, you must break through your comfort zone and do things that are not comfortable.

—T. Harv Eker

We must lean toward the miracles we want to manifest. Success takes sacrifice, but try not to interpret sacrifice as subtraction—that you have to lose things to get things. Sacrifice is actually more like addition. We are simply going to be adding more time and attention to achieving the things we want. The more we achieve, the more we experience the additions to our lives that we desire. For instance, we don't lose anything in having children. The process of raising children adds only an increase in richness, love, direction, hard work, and abundance to our lives. Anything we love requires our time, love, and attention. To succeed at anything, we have to actively, consciously, and purposefully show up. We have to be consistent and excited about what we're doing. When we hit the phases where we cannot stand what we're doing anymore, we must do those things anyway. There is no path to miracles that can come through any form of laziness, fear, or procrastination. When our beliefs are deep enough in what we're doing, we just do it. We have to do it. We must be the type of person who cannot imagine not doing it, not putting a meaningful piece of ourselves into this world.

What is the real price we pay for our dreams? Personal growth, excitement, joy, love, passion, nice things, vacations, contributing, giving, and truly living. How bad can that be? These all sound like rewards to me. They are all additions, not subtractions.

Focus on Action, Not Comparison

Preparation and action can be easily and unnecessarily halted when we compare ourselves to others. The more successful we become, we elevate ourselves into groups of more successful people.

When we have an idea and the passion to grow it, we succeed to levels we could have never imagined. Each new level of success will bring out a natural feeling of being overwhelmed. Because each level of our process is new, the terrain is always changing. Wherever there is change, there is doubt. We may question if we really have what it takes to continue expanding and moving up. We may feel insecure that we won't or don't fit with the other successes at this new level. The other successful people around us may speak a language of success we have yet to hear or experience. Whatever it is, all we have to do is observe, trust, listen, and learn. To leverage feelings of insecurity or intimidation, it is helpful to take our focus from what is outward to what is inward. We must go inward and take refuge within our own being and process what we can do as an individual to adjust and take care of our next steps forward. Fear will be a part of any meaningful process. We can let fear sneak up from behind, engulf us, and hold us back, or we can imagine the hands of fear being placed gently upon our lower back and pushing us courageously forward. Fear is an energy. It can be a useful energy when we utilize it as a motivational force. Our fears help us identify where the holes in our plans are, giving us clues regarding where we need to further grow and prepare.

Getting out of our comfort zone is always a challenging and difficult transition but well worth it. To prepare for the next leap, we must examine our fearful tendencies. Do we go from believing that we can reach our goals to feeling totally hopeless and defeated? If we have such a swing in our thoughts, we need to take more time to prepare and secure any insecurity leaks in our plan. If we are always thinking negatively, how can we expect to create a successful and joyful life for ourselves?

Preparation is a function of how we think and what we do. What we tell ourselves every day has a deep and direct impact on what happens in our lives. If we want to take action, to be fearless, we have to make the necessary positive changes in ourselves. We must believe that increase and opportunity are not things that run out. Rather, they are always possible for us. We must use fear as the fuel to continue our movement forward. We can look at fear as our greatest competitor: one that we *want* chasing us to make us go faster, not the competitor who is in front of us holding us back. If we make sure to stay one step ahead of fear, we are guaranteed to come out victorious. It's always good to have a worthy competitor to keep us on our toes; for this reason, we must thank our fears.

Coachable Moment

Procrastination is one of the most common and deadliest of diseases and its toll on success and happiness is heavy.

–*Wayne Gretzky*

Take the Action of Involving Others in Your Journey

The whole purpose of our lives is to add value to them as well as to the lives of others. We need other people, and it's important to humble ourselves to this truth. Coming together, bringing people together, sharing, and contributing are the elements that make being a human being so remarkable and special. Serving others rather than just ourselves matters. No one in this life accomplishes anything worthwhile all on their own. To be great at what we do, we need to focus on providing the guidance, tools, and training necessary to help others become even better, and we must invite better, more successful others into our lives to help us become better. When we learn to put people first, they will put our mission first because they will feel supported and nurtured to do their work. In making others feel valued, the mission we are on becomes valued. There isn't a driven human being who doesn't want to feel important and to believe that he or she is involved in something extraordinary. When we have a group of people supporting us and we view our purpose to be one of helping and involving as many other people as possible, taking action each day is driven by love rather than labor.

The mind-set of action I encourage you to have is this: *I will do one thing every day that no one else is willing to do. Just one. Even if it's simple. Even if it's small.* If you commit to just doing this, I can guarantee that after a week you'll be uncommon, after a month you'll be special, and after a year you'll be extraordinary.

Do all you can to build lasting connections. Involve others in your mission. Focus on developing real connections instead of "getting numbers." Needs for safety and security come with relationships generating a sense of community. You need real connections: people you can help, people you can trust, people who can help you, and people who genuinely care about other people.

When you make lasting connections, you create an extended professional family—a group of like-minded people who have the same heart and desire to give something extraordinary of themselves to the world. Supported by these intentions and connections, you will absolutely have the security necessary to succeed. When you involve others in your journey, you have the joy of accountability motivating you to stay committed and determined because others are counting on you.

Fearlessness
Belief + Action = FEARLESSNESS

There is no result without preparation.

Preparation is education.

Preparation is knowledge backed with research.

Preparation is what gives us the courage to create measurable momentum toward a goal.

Preparation provides the proof we need to back our beliefs.

Preparation builds confidence.

When our beliefs can be proven as valid through our research, we can move to the next phase of executing our mission. Preparation gives us the platform of fearlessness we need to stand on to continue moving up the ladder of success.

For our actions to be clear, our beliefs must be strong. This is *fearlessness*. And fearlessness requires preparation, for preparation defeats fear. You must train yourself to feel the fear of what is ahead of you and do what needs to be done in spite of those fears. It takes a touch of madness to be successful. Each new level of success will have its own set of fears for you to face and surpass to keep your vision growing. Whether you fail or succeed, you learn and grow. Growth, in and of itself, is a form of preparation that leaves all doors to your success wide open. You can even return to doors that had previously been closed on you and knock again when you're properly prepared to deliver what you were unable to before. Preparation builds enough belief for you to take action again and again.

We must be willing to dare greatly in our lives. Fearlessness is not a little thing. It takes incredible courage to love fully, to change ourselves when necessary, to feel deeply, to leave situations and relationships when it's scary, and to chase our dreams fearlessly and with an unwavering tenacity. To become fearless, we must put action behind our beliefs and include like-minded others in our mission. Fearlessness isn't a measure of what we say but rather a measure of what we do.

MARINATE ON THIS

If you're not willing to risk the unusual,
you will have to settle for the ordinary.

—*Jim Rohn*

Grace + Strategy = Execution

*Some people want it to happen, some wish
it would happen, others make it happen.*
—Michael Jordan

elf-awareness.

The ability to think rationally.

A strong sense of security.

Each of these aspects of self-awareness helps us show grace under pressure.

And each helps us think clearly enough to develop strategies for life and business that are authentic to who we are.

It is our failures, hardships, and the strong foundation of the strength of our purpose that give us the fitness necessary to succeed. Add to that our willingness to take action and we have the tools we need to survive and thrive. Our failures and hardships create the firm foundation we confidently stand upon. This foundation provides us the courage, fitness, and depth of purpose required for our success. When we have these elements in place, we come more naturally to the willingness to take action because we feel secure that we possess the tools we need to thrive.

Never do we come to know who we really are or what we're capable of overcoming until we have experienced the pressures and fears of failure. These pressures are what force us to be scrappy, brave, and persistent. It is through our trials that we develop the grace and maturity necessary to believe that all things will fall perfectly into place as long as we endure.

When we are clear about our directions, have prepared well thought-out strategies, and put the required action behind them, we have what is called *execution*. Execution is different than action. Execution is bigger and geared more toward the end result we desire, whereas action is more acute, geared toward the now, and contains all the small steps we need to take to create our bigger picture. Each successful action we execute builds our confidence. This confidence makes us fearless enough for our bigger execution phases.

When we execute, we release our knowledge into the world in a meaningful and direct way. We want our strategies of execution to be a reflection of our integrity, knowledge, work ethic, and good character. If we are sound people, we will create sound strategies to realize our dreams. The quality of how we execute is like a business card: it says something about who we are, the way we think, the depth of our beliefs, how well prepared we are, how willing we are to risk, and how innovative we are in achieving our goals. We each have the choice to execute from a mind-set of class, integrity, and grace or from a mind-set of greed and sheer opportunism. How well we execute is a reflection of how well we know ourselves and value our reputation.

GRACE

GRACE + Strategy = Execution

What is grace? Grace is a measure of staying calm under pressure.

Why is having grace integral to success and longevity? The more fear, failure, and heartbreak we overcome, the more grace we develop.

Grace is a reflection of our competence. It is that fixed state of mind that carries us with more ease through life's problems, obstacles, and difficult communications. It is that quality in us that stands out when we are living in that sweet space of things flowing effortlessly. There is no good reason for us to live with a sense of entitlement or with big egos. When we have grace, our focus is on faith and gratitude. We don't complain about our more fearful situations. Instead we take time to better prepare. Grace gives us a tangible aura of elegance and is developed through the processes of communicating, networking, growing, staying fit, and developing our self-awareness to greater depths as we grow and succeed. Put another way, grace is a reflection of our maturity and the depth of our life experience. When we have grace, we naturally move in a strong and self-assured manner because we know who we are. We approach life with a purity of sophistication. We realize that we have experienced some failure along the way, but we also know that we have grown and found our way through it. All of our life experiences develop who we are; we move forward knowing this and acting on its truth.

When we live our lives focused on triumph, patience, and faith, we naturally hold good physical posture and act with vulnerability and self-assurance because we know who we are. We have not given up regardless of the odds we have faced. Grace expresses the undeniable quality of our well-earned wisdom.

The more success we experience, the more of a responsibility we have to live our lives with grace. Egotistical "successes" are not really successes at all. They are only superficially successful. Without emotional, mental, and spiritual depth, there may be some elements of success, but there cannot be wealth. Wealth is a much deeper and more meaningful experience than being rich and famous.

To maintain a state of grace, we must be attuned to those times and circumstances when it's in our best interest to step back and just take a moment. It's incredibly settling to our reactive nature to take a step back when feeling stressed and just breathe deeply for a few minutes. Oxygen helps our brain process emotion. When we are in fight-or-flight mode, the brain receives less oxygen because we tend to take shorter and shallower breaths. When we force ourselves to take a few deep breaths before reacting, we counteract the body's natural reaction to the stressful situation. When we inhale deeply and exhale slowly, it grounds us to the present moment, allowing us to anchor our thought process. As the oxygen floods the brain, emotions settle and thoughts become more rational. As we breathe, we begin to feel calm and collected. Being calm takes our mind-set from emergency mode into reality where we can discover sound solutions. This is what we learn from facing and surpassing our fears. And this is where we learn to have grace under fire.

Coachable Moment

Integrity is choosing your thoughts and actions based on value rather than personal gain.

—*Anonymous*

Visualize the Positive

Like any virtue, living with grace waxes and wanes. When we lose our sense of grace, one surefire way to restore it is to train ourselves to visualize the possibility. When pressures are intense, it is easy to focus only on the adversity at hand, lose our sense of grace, and become stuck in the negative thoughts of what could happen if our problem isn't quickly solved. Grace and rushing cannot coexist, so to maintain our composure, we must learn to take inventory of how far we have come and how many obstacles we have surpassed. And then we need to ground ourselves in that deep trust we have in ourselves to handle our situations with intelligence, determination, preparation, and success.

To derail doubts, fears, and other forms of emotional chaos, you need to take a moment to close your eyes. Focus on the mental image of the outcome you would like to see in response to the adversity you're facing. Visualize solutions coming in and solving the problem. Imagine the emotional satisfaction you feel as you visualize yourself succeeding and moving past the triggering issue. It is well worth it to take time in this way to direct your thoughts toward a successful resolution. It will help restore you to a place of grace. Using visualization in this way will anchor you.

I also suggest engaging in positive and reassuring self-talk as you visualize. When feeling fearful, give yourself a pep talk, review your goals, and remind yourself of how prepared and knowledgeable you are to handle the obstacle you are facing. Stress is caused by fear. Fear is not a thing. It is just a thought. Once you get a handle on the anxiety that's provoking the thoughts flooding your psyche, the fear goes as well. Pause to execute until you can execute from the steadiness of grace. It is vital that you listen to the advice you give yourself and live it out.

Talk yourself into success.

Talk yourself into greatness.

Talk yourself into confidence.

Envision yourself handling all situations with grace—and you will.

Coachable Moment
The most important conversation you can
have is the one you have with yourself.
—Jim Rohn

Treat Others with Grace

Grace is most noticeable in how we treat others and handle conflict. And as we learned in the last equation, we must include others in our mission. This requires grace and inclusion.

We must strive to be inclusive. Being inclusive means seeing beyond external differences by choosing to look into the soul of each person. Treating others with grace means not prejudging. It means having the capacity to place another person's needs over our own. People are looking to have their emotional needs taken care of, not manipulated. We must never sell anyone a false bag of goods. In fact, when we have grace, there is no need to *sell* ourselves at all. With grace, we possess the integrity to *present* ourselves as authentically as we are and in the truth of what we have to offer.

To be successful, we must appreciate all people. We must care for every human being and demonstrate this in our approach to the world. We must choose collaboration over competition. Sustaining success is about appreciating what *all* people bring to the table. We must strive to be a token of peace.

If we are to operate with grace, we must be trustworthy. If we are not genuine, if we are hiding who we are and harboring a set of secret agendas about what we want to get from others, we reduce ourselves to a false set of pretenses. People can feel this. We have all been around that person who is "too nice," and we know it's not real. We instinctively feel we cannot trust this person because their niceness is so sickly sweet it repulses us. We immediately sense a secret agenda behind their display of false emotion that is manipulative and selfish and causes us to reflexively back away and self-protect. On the other hand, we respond the most positively to others, and others to us, when we are being fully authentic to who we are.

Moreover, we must respect others to gain their respect in return. I have always been prejudged. For many people, I apparently don't fit the typical image of a woman who is a psychologist or business writer or someone with a doctorate. I have always been underestimated. In fact, during one of my doctoral residencies, the supervisor was teaching us to be careful not to judge a book by its cover when starting treatment with a new patient. The example he used in front of thirty other doctoral students was "Look at Sherrie Campbell. If we judged a book by its cover, we would never assume she was smart, let alone have a PhD and to be one of our top residents." I am grateful to have a flexible, light-hearted sense of humor so I could roll with what he said. In some strange way, I realized he offered me a compliment, though he had done it in terribly poor taste. The judgment of me as "not smart" was disrespectful and unfair to me. Still, I suppose my supervisor was trying to convey that we cannot judge or diagnose our new patients before spending time with them. The lesson is: when we show respect to others—meaning, we remain open to them before assuming anything about them—we set the tone for others to be more open to and less judgmental toward us.

Whenever people are placed in a position to earn our trust, we place them in a position to be judged. This is not respectful but egotistical. We must give all people the room to reveal their true nature. When or if they prove to be unkind or untrustworthy, we activate our decision-making to rid our lives of these types. It takes time for people to reveal themselves as most of us put our best face forward in the beginning of any new venture or relationship. Time and experience with others will tell us everything we need to know to make the best decisions we can about them, for them, and most importantly for our own success and self-care. When we operate from grace, from giving others a fair amount of time to show their character, we never demand respect but give it. We need to give others the grace and time they deserve so if trust is lost, it is lost because of a real cause rather than by a false and unfair judgment. We tend to judge those who are different than us. For example, physically disabled people are often judged as mentally impaired too, which is rarely the case. Too often they feel as if they have to prove themselves, unfairly, just because they are different than other people. We must be open to differences and offer fairness. When we view others from a place of equality, we provide the space for everyone to feel respected, needed, and included.

Inclusion should not be threatening to us if we come from a place of ethics. Achieving success cannot be all about business and earning; it must also be about being a good human being. We must be open to others.

Coachable Moment

Goodness is about character— integrity, honesty, kindness, generosity, moral courage, and the like. More than anything else, it is about how we treat other people.

—Dennis Prager

Personal Grace

To operate with a sense of personal grace, we have to accept that bad things happen. Neither life nor business will ever be perfect. There will undoubtedly be ups and downs in our personal and business lives, with one directly impacting the other. With acceptance comes grace. When we accept the natural ebb and flow of attention, abundance, energy, and focus, we adjust with more ease to changing conditions. We must develop systems, practices, and networks to help provide us with a sense of continuity and security. When we have security, we naturally operate with more grace because we live from a strong and trusted sense of safety. When change is happening, it is easy to lose our grace and get caught up in fear and anxiety, which only make our complex situations more chaotic. However, as we learn to be comfortable in our transitions, to take the necessary time to observe our reactions, thoughts, and fears, we train ourselves to stay on a more stable course.

Part of having personal grace means having the courage and willingness to thoroughly address personal issues that inhibit our happiness and success. This often means seeking personal therapy, hiring a business coach, paying off old debts, or starting a new exercise program or dietary regimen. We know from the equation on peak performance how important it is to live a clean and healthy life. To feel grace operating through our lives, we must like who we are and how it feels to be who we are physically, emotionally, mentally, and spiritually. We must take time to listen to all aspects of our life. We must listen intently to our heart, our intuition, our body, our spirit, and what others are telling us. We need this kind of feedback from our physical and social environments. All the answers we need are available if we listen. And then we must trust the answers, take action, and put them into place. We cannot live in a chaotic and reactive state of mind and be graceful in our lives. When we live with grace, we love ourselves, we love our lives, and we engage in the consistent process of raising our standards.

In a world dominated by extroversion, living with grace has become something of a rarity. Many people are practically yelling their answers and opinions out into the world in an effort to be the most noticed and the first to speak. The advent of social media and the selfie have brought a whole new genre of attention seeking. However, we garner more respect when we choose to listen more than we speak. We must strive to operate from a quiet spirit of intelligence and experience. We must make it our intention to be persons of great dignity rather than persons with the loudest volume. There is nothing appealing about a showoff.

Think about the word *grace*. What does it inspire? How would a person of grace operate in life and business?

Having grace is the most powerful character trait to possess when looking to advance our lives. Our personal grace represents the essence of who we are.

Here are the character traits of grace we must work to assimilate into our own personalities to increase our chances at succeeding.

Self-assurance

Grace comes from knowing who we are and is a reflection of what we believe about ourselves. We must choose to believe we are capable of handling any problem presented to us. This belief is the foundation for our success. When we are self-assured, people get the vibe that we like, respect, appreciate, and value who we are and what we bring to any situation, need, or task. It is so important that we know our value, appreciate our talents, and show a steady work ethic.

When we operate from such a spirit of grace, we are taken more seriously. It makes others curious about who we are and our thoughts on life and business. After all, we can either *affect* people or *infect* them. It takes grace to positively affect the goodness in others in contrast to manipulation, which infects them. How much better it is to act from a standpoint of self-assured grace.

Hopefulness

It is impossible to be panicky and graceful at the same time. We must deeply believe there are solutions for every problem. We don't need to panic on the way to discovering solutions. Our frustrations block innovation. But as we cultivate a hopeful outlook, solutions come easier and with less effort.

Hopefulness requires faith in ourselves and faith in our future. When we live with hope-filled grace, we must discipline ourselves to operate from a mind-set of faithfulness. When we have faith, people are drawn to us. The strength of our faith makes others feel more hopeful. It makes being in our company a positive experience.

Responsibility

Whatever happens in our careers or relationships, the most efficient way to practice grace is to accept responsibility for the outcomes, both positive and negative, which result from our efforts. If we make a mistake, we must view it as a self-created learning experience. We must humble ourselves, admit wrong, take ownership, and make the necessary changes. Grace is not about ego. It is about humility and a willingness to learn. When we're mature enough to take responsibility for our outcomes, this will inspire the willingness in others to accept responsibility for the outcomes of their lives.

Kindness

There is no greater virtue to possess as a human being than the simple power of kindness. Kindness does not mean you are a yes person or a pushover. Kindness is based in empathy and in the desire to understand others. It is the place we speak from where both good and bad news are communicated with an evenness of temper. When we live with grace, we use kindness as our approach to giving feedback. We are wise to understand that kindness is our greatest relationship-building and networking tool because it creates an emotional environment advantageous to all who are able to be a part of it.

Poise under pressure

When we have grace, we are able to self-regulate when we are emotional. We make sure to process our emotions before communicating as a way to avoid speaking too soon and inadvertently causing irreparable damage to significant relationships. When we operate with empathic accuracy, successful interactions with others are nearly guaranteed. With grace, we possess the depth and awareness to predict the attitudes, expectations, and intentions of others. This type of predictability creates an interpersonal connectedness between us and our awareness of others that helps our relationships to succeed and thrive. We leave others feeling heard, validated, and understood.

Thoughtfulness

Thoughtfulness is at the heart of grace. We must be thoughtful, not just to benefit ourselves but largely for the benefit of others. We must care about how we are received as well as how others feel in our presence.

Thoughtfulness requires that we choose our words wisely and project an attitude and posture of self-respect and intelligence.

We must learn to operate in an unhurried manner, which shows thoughtfulness at work.

We must be thoughtful to fully educate ourselves in our field of expertise and to provide the information or data necessary to those who need it. We must be unselfish with our knowledge.

When interacting with others, we must make sure we are mindful of our tone, our volume, and the image we project. Each of us needs to be a person who chooses to build positive, supportive, and trusting networks. Thoughtfulness is the one characteristic that guarantees no one will ever be sold short when in our presence.

Self-possession

Self-possession, or the ability to remain composed, is another key element to our success. It puts us in direct control of ourselves. With grace, we give ourselves time to choose how we respond to any given event rather than getting emotionally hijacked. When we live with self-possession, we stay mindful to what is important regardless of temporary pressures or temptations. Self-possession increases the all-important virtue of tolerance. It gives us the foresight to expect obstacles and deal with them diplomatically. When we expect challenge, we respond with more courage, strength, and optimism. We understand that emotional discomfort is an integral part of any important endeavor; therefore, we don't add any additional suffering, bitterness, or revenge to the mix by losing hold on ourselves. Instead, we roll up our sleeves and do the work we need to do.

When we practice the different mind-sets that make up grace, we cultivate our personal excellence. There is nothing more gratifying than striving for greatness with a sense of humility. We must desire to have our reputation based on the quality of our work and on the exemplary qualities we possess as a human being rather than becoming well known for being loud, bullish, and self-centered. Composure inspires us to seek respect rather than attention because we know respect lasts much longer.

Grace in the Face of Rejection

Can we have grace in the face of rejection? Yes! Remember that *acceptance* piece of the puzzle we discussed previously? To be successful, we have to accept that we can't win them all. That's just life. It can be extremely painful and difficult to be gracious when we experience failure or rejection. However, when we ignite grace, we show the depth of our character. When we demonstrate grace in the face of a rejection, we make ourselves unforgettable to others, but more importantly, strong as steel within ourselves.

Always thank those who reject you for the opportunity that was at hand. When you do this, it showcases your class and integrity. Internally you must remind yourself that losing and winning are both guarantees in life. Not all opportunities are meant to be yours and that's okay. This can be a tough pill to swallow, and sometimes it's incredibly hard to move beyond not getting something you want, but it doesn't help to throw a tantrum, confront, criticize, or create conflict with those who have turned you down. A great way to move beyond these moments is to do so with a gracious and humble acceptance of the result in the presence of those who are turning you away. This allows you to leave with your pride and trusting you will be remembered for your exceptional maturity.

A great way to coach yourself through these rejections is to try to trust that this only brings you one step closer to the yes you are seeking. I always tell myself that all things are happening perfectly for me or something different would be happening. This helps ease the sting of the rejection so I can move toward letting that opportunity go while starting to look for what is next. There is always something next. I would rather look for what is next than stay stuck in what I didn't get. I have a dogged refusal to be defined by who or what rejected me. I make sure to define myself by how strongly I move on and how steadily I have the power to emerge from the depths with a new ace to play.

Coachable Moment

I take rejection as someone blowing a bugle in my ear to wake me up and get going, rather than retreat.

—Sylvester Stallone

STRATEGY

Grace + STRATEGY = Solutions

To effectively strategize, we must always consider our bigger picture, and grace is part of this consideration. Without a sense of grace, there is no path to strategic thinking.

Strategic thinking is the mental process we apply to our desire to succeed. It's human to be tempted to deal with what is immediate because the immediate seems more urgent and concrete. Unfortunately, if we do this, we put our path to success at great risk. If we allow ourselves to become overly focused on potholes, we end up missing the bonus opportunities, not to mention any signals that the road we're on may be leading us off a cliff. Potholes are immediate, as they are right in front of you and act as irritants or pebbles in our shoes that distract us from our bigger picture. For instance, when we're in an airplane and hit turbulence, if the turbulence is all we focus on, the flight will be miserable and scary. However, when we shift our attention to the destination we are traveling to (the bigger picture), a little instability and shaking are easier to tolerate. Where we are going makes a little turbulence well worth it. This is a tough job—make no mistake about it. But this is why we must practice becoming great strategists.

The Way of the Strategic Thinker

The majority of us focus on what is directly in front of us. But this approach is usually narrow-minded and lacks peripheral vision. It leaves us vulnerable to rivals who are likely more adept at detecting and acting on the more ambiguous signals. When things are unclear, we must not wait or be inattentive or lazy until the needed information shows up. We must not ignore what is ambiguous but rather look to find the information to fill the whole. This is how we learn to stay ahead of the competition, to live on the cutting edge, and to function being outside of our comfort zone. If we want to be the best at what we do, we must embrace being active discoverers of our own answers. To anticipate well, we must look for the game-changing information that only exists at the cutting edge of our industry. In other words, we must be willing to think out of the box and explore new thought. One great way to do this is to build vast external networks to help us better scan our horizons. The larger we expand our networks, the more information we gain from the edges. This information then helps us anticipate and devise our next successful move.

Thinking critically is vital to developing great strategy, yet most of us think in habituated patterns, which is why expanding to the edges is necessary. Certainly, our more predictable insights provoke less risk to raised eyebrows and second-guessing from our peers, but this way is too safe. We must avoid parroting every new business fad if we desire to develop a more competitive edge.

Rather than simply following the crowd, train yourself to question everything. To develop this type of thinking and bravery, you must learn to reframe your problems and work to get to the root cause. Be willing to challenge your individual and collective beliefs. Be willing to change your mind-set whenever necessary as a way to uncover any hypocrisy, manipulation, and bias in the decisions you choose to make.

Also strive to never be predictable. A great strategist does not spend days trying to play the role that others have chosen for him or her.

The greatest strategy you have is to be authentic. Get into a mind-set where you can trust your own brilliance. This means you must believe in your own voice, your own story, and the power of your own words, decisions, and purpose.

Be Excited about Ambiguity

We must train ourselves to embrace ambiguity rather than resist it.

Ambiguity, at the very least, brings anticipation and excitement. It forces us to interpret the overall culture of the situation we're in. When things are ambiguous, we are the most tempted to reach for an anchor—any shortsighted, quick-fix solution to return to feelings of safety. The psyche struggles against uncertainty. To become a great strategist, we must hold our grace, and practice self-control. To come up with the most effective strategies, we must utilize the time available to carefully analyze and interpret the patterns of behavior in front of us and to assimilate multiple sources of information before choosing to execute. We do this through the use of the success formulas explained in this book. We must draw upon the boldness of our vision, our fitness, our keen sense of self-awareness, the fearlessness we've developed to take action, and finally the intelligence to know when and how to best execute. The most exhilarating thing about ambiguity is each time we make a decision, we must execute from a touch of blind insanity. We must learn to balance every move we make with speed, rigor, quality, agility, and a certain level of detachment. We must be willing to take a stand even when we realize we do not have all the information we need. This takes tremendous courage.

Coachable Moment

If you are unsure of a course of action, do not attempt it. Your doubts and hesitations will infect your execution. Timidity is dangerous: Better to enter with boldness. Any mistakes you commit through audacity are easily corrected with more audacity. Everyone admires the bold; no one honors the timid.

—Robert Greene

To be great strategists, we must understand that agreement or consensus is rare whenever making decisions. Therefore, it is important to create open communication within our network—communication that builds trust and engages key people, especially when viewpoints are different. To pull that off, we have to possess a depth of understanding of what drives other people's agendas, including what they choose not to reveal.

When I am working with patients, it is imperative I understand the problem, their obstacles, the needs they are looking to fulfill, and what lies below the surface psychologically that may be holding them back. I have found that it is my own self-awareness that helps me see what is revealed as well as the issues that still lie below the surface in a state of fear, shame, or insecurity. A little probing into my clients' emotions helps me understand what motivates them and how to get them beyond their insecurities into a place of feeling happier and more confident. We cannot do that work without self-awareness. Self-awareness and grace help us bring tough issues to the surface when things are uncomfortable.

It's also true that all great strategists are dedicated learners. As our success grows, honest feedback is harder to come by; therefore, we have to do whatever we can to keep it coming. No matter how difficult the objective, we must trust there are ways to overcome our obstacles through obtaining the feedback and support we need. Communication helps us more accurately analyze the capacity for risk and follow-through. This helps us acquire the necessary supports to execute on decisions made.

I believe and have personally discovered that you must have the capacity to live with a touch of reckless abandon to successfully navigate the pursuit of happiness and success. You must be graceful enough to live in the truth of things, even when that truth hurts. Feedback is crucial because success and failure, especially failure, are valuable sources of learning. To ensure honest feedback, encourage it in those around you by modeling it yourself. You have to be willing and courageous enough to shift course quickly when you realize you're missing the mark and only banging your head against the same wall over and over. Changing course can be scary, but it is the excitement you get from the more ambiguous parts of your journey that equip you with the deepest growth. Honor these times. Let them stretch you. They will guide you to true wealth.

Do You Have What It Takes? Yes ... You Do!

The strongest emotion backing any successful strategy is passion. And passion requires courage to express it and follow it wherever it may lead.

There is nothing more intoxicating than a person full of passion. Just look at Tony Robbins and his impact on the world. He is perhaps the most well known motivational speaker on planet Earth. He has overcome incredible odds in life and teaches us by his own example that anything—absolutely anything—is also possible for each and every one of us.

We must be creative enough to throw ourselves unhesitatingly into the river of the passion flowing through our hearts. If we are not passionate about what we do, the risk will not be rewarding. We must be passionate enough to feel and choose our own desires.

To be a great strategist we must be willing to border on the edge of great risk, but we must also be wise enough not to rely on the power of passion alone. To develop strategies that go beyond passion, we must learn to make use of our competitor's energy as much as our own. Whenever we enter into a negotiation, it's important to make use of our excitement and passion, especially since emotions are contagious. The passion we have may be enough for some to want to join in on our mission.

However, as negotiations progress, we may find that our excitement and passion are inadequate to persuade some of those we're desiring to influence. To add to this then, we must rely on our experience, research, and the evidence we've gathered to secure what we need to keep moving forward. Without passion, experience, and evidence, there is no amount of skill or talent that will provide us with the impact we envision. To be great with strategy, we cannot just be a loud mouth with a great idea. We must also be smart, prepared, and able to predict what questions we may be asked. We must have the information necessary to give sound answers. If we don't have the answers we need to secure the next phase of execution, then we must learn to bide our time till we do.

When pushed, some individuals would rather lie than let it be known that they have run out of answers. They don't want to be embarrassed or miss their opportunity so they offer made-up information instead of admitting they need time to gather the missing information. While expedient, this approach to overcoming the obstacle is unnecessary and detrimental. A great strategist never resorts to the use of dishonesty. It is better to use tactics such as delay or distraction in lieu of dishonesty. To maintain the integrity of your reputation, you must commit to always being honest. No matter how anxious you may be, you must use other strategies at your disposal to gain your objective. When you feel that your answers are not going to come to mind, let your competitors know that you need more time to get them what they're requesting.

There are times when being vague while gathering our evidence is the key to successfully negotiating. Curiosity breeds interest. Vague is not meant to reference any form of dishonesty. When you are negotiating to win, it is not always wise to put all your cards on the table. As a competitive athlete, whenever we were creating a new competition routine, my coaches and I kept my new skills and what music I would be performing quiet until competition time. I have memories of being asked what jumps I could land and how many of those jumps would be in my new program. I always bid for more time by saying that my routine was not yet set, that it was still subject to change, which was true. But I would not answer questions with specifics. I remained vague because I wanted my new skills, as showcased in my new routine, to be a surprise when I finally used them in my performance.

Never be dishonest. Instead, ask for more time. In the process, you may even come up with an even bigger deal than the one you initially presented. And if you're confident you will, you can even mention that in negotiations. Whenever possible, you want to leave others convinced they will gain more in joining your mission than if they didn't.

Learning and growing are invigorating. To be great strategists, we must ask a ton of questions, become avid researchers and active thinkers. To live lives we love, we must take advantage of every opportunity we have to connect with people heart-to-heart, vision-to-vision. When we love what we are pursuing, we have a natural gleam in our eyes, and we truly hunger for the new information that will help change our lives even more.

As we travel along our path, we will also undoubtedly experience times of suffering. It's how life is. We will find ourselves consumed with unkind and vengeful thoughts and sometimes believe we are totally incapable of growing. We will oftentimes, out of frustration, deem ourselves unworthy of any blessing or miracle, especially when we seem at a loss for the evidence or information we need to move forward. We will fluctuate in and out of feeling sure of what our purpose is and even if we're on the right track. To be great, we will hold many meetings with suffering where we will question and experience great doubt and deep fear. We should expect to spend many sleepless nights believing that our strategies are ridiculous, and that without something better our lives will not have the meaning we are searching for. Yet, it is our mistakes and the dark trespasses through these lost feelings that are the exact things which grow us into great strategists. Our mistakes make us question ourselves. They force the hand of our ability to problem-solve and be resilient. However, because we question, because we're looking for understanding, we will eventually find it. Wisdom is what suffering looks like once it's healed.

Strategy is a measure of how we get to those higher aims in ourselves and our relationships while under the umbrella of uncertainty. We have to possess the personal grace and clarity to be attuned to patterns and to discover new ways of achieving what we want. To have what it takes, we cannot lose sight of things that last or the strong bonds we have forged over time that have gotten us this far. We must be able to distinguish between what is transient and what is enduring. For this reason, we must always remain in touch with how much we each have to be thankful for. When we are grateful for our lives and careers, things tend to fall into place at the right time, giving us access to the faith we need to believe that, no matter how uncertain things may seem, they are ultimately working out in our favor.

I suggest that, at the end of each day, you kneel in gratitude for the positivity and success you have in your life. Choose never to be a person who needs to be reminded of how others have helped you. You must be the first to remember and make sure to share the rewards and accolades you receive with those who have helped you get to where you are today. None of us succeeds alone.

∽◟∕∕◞

Coachable Moment

All great people of history, all the heroes and leaders and innovators who lit humanity's way out of darkness and ignorance, forged within themselves the courage to overcome their internal conflicts when it mattered most. In many ways, they are just like us: They worried. They procrastinated. They sometimes had lower opinions of their fellow human beings. But what made them celebrated, what pushed society forward, what gave birth to their legend, was their sheer will to overcome such impulses and to faithfully, actively, and lovingly fight for a better life for themselves and others. Let us learn from them, let us master ourselves, and let us now add our own chapter of courage to the good book of humanity.

—*Brendon Burchard*

EXECUTION
Grace + Strategy = EXECUTION

While strategy is important, execution is everything. Strategy is not a product. Binders are filled with strategies that were never implemented. A strategy must be actualized. And that's the role of execution.

To execute, we have to start with our first success equation and develop an idea or a vision. Once we have this, we can create a strategy and set up systems of operation to make our foundations strong, safe, and secure. Execution, then, launches our vision. When we have the steadiness of our personal grace, intelligent strategies, and the evidence we need to press forward toward our bigger picture, we are ready for takeoff.

Once strategies have been executed, we face the unexpected since there is no way to guarantee what the results will be. After we execute, we must adapt, learn, flex, and learn. For this reason, we should bless each moment of uncertainty. We must remind ourselves that desperation kills strategy and eliminates solutions. When we approach uncertainty with rigor, grace, and the clarity of what it takes to create great strategies, we develop the successful executions that build our bigger picture.

Successful execution is what takes us to new places, to new levels, and into new and even more dynamic relationships. As we begin to experience the fruits of our labor, as accumulated through successful executions, we begin to need more than just success. Success means nothing if it is not shared. The more we succeed, we develop an even deeper need to share our experiences with others.

MARINATE ON THIS

There are really three parts to the creative process. First there is inspiration, then there is the execution, and finally there is the release.

—*Eddie Van Halen*

Part 3

LOVE AND
BELONGING NEEDS

We must understand love; we must be able to teach it, to create it, to predict it, or else the world is lost to hostility and to suspicion.
—Abraham Maslow

Human beings are social animals, and by our nature we seek companionship, acceptance, and inclusion. Maslow identifies love and belonging needs as basic requirements for friendships, peer support, and the ability to give and receive love. The workplace offers us the extraordinary opportunity to be a part of a team in which each member shares ideas, personal knowledge, perspectives, skills, and unique life experiences to solve problems in which they have a vested interest. We desire to be a part of teams, families, and other inner circles that give us a sense of our own place in the mix as leaders, followers, learners, and growers. Being social also provides us with competitors, focus groups, brainstorming sessions, after-work get-togethers, and even office potlucks that make employees feel as if they are "family."

Love + Healthy Boundaries = Emotional Security

There are two basic motivating forces: fear and love. When we are afraid, we pull back from life. When we are in love, we open to all that life has to offer with passion, excitement, and acceptance.

—John Lennon

Love is the most powerful force in existence.

Love brings us a sense of security, belonging, safety, and connection. When we feel loved, we are more confident. When we feel loved, we are happier, more fulfilled, more secure, and therefore more courageous. I can tell you without reservation that the loves I am so blessed to have in my life are a large part of the reason I strive so hard to succeed, but more importantly, they make me want to be a better person. It is much easier to go through life with people who forecast your needs, support you, understand you, and help fill your life with hope, love, and possibility. When we have this type of foundation, we have a place to spring forth from and a place to return to, regardless of our results. This is love.

Love is the foundation that acts as our safe-base in life. It's the place we can return to, whether life has been good or bad to us on any particular day. We can find rest for our soul in love's comfort.

There is no greater force to work from or for than love.

When we have love, we have proof we exist and that we are significant and necessary.

To succeed, we must love who we are. We must love the people in our lives. We must love what we do. We must love working.

Love is a motivation, a need, and a drive. It is what gives everything in our lives meaning and purpose. In fact, without love, life has no purpose. A person without love or purpose becomes corrupt. As Eminem says, "Love spelled backwards is Evol." With love, we change for the better.

I know this with certainty: When we love our lives, our lives will love us back.

Love

LOVE + Healthy Boundaries = Emotional Security

As basic and important as love is, it certainly isn't simple. I know it doesn't sound very romantic, but love is a verb (action) as well as an emotion. Love is something we *do* as much as something we *feel*. Love has to be reciprocal and active for it to grow and sustain. We all want love to last, so we must be willing to work at love just as hard as we work in other areas of our lives. People who don't know how to *do* love—to both give and receive it—lose love and pick up bitterness.

At its core, love is about sharing. And sharing involves being considerate of others and being consistent with who we say we are. I truly believe that how we show and express our love is the greatest statement of who we are. If we are self-centered, this will come out in the way we love. With love, we must be willing to be unselfish, especially when it would be easier not to be.

In my romantic relationship, we try to hold "company" meetings every four to six weeks. During these meetings, which usually occur while we're hiking or out to dinner, we each put items on the table about what is working in our relationship and which items need some adjusting. We allow ourselves to be vulnerable so we can find the truth about where the middle ground exists between us. This vulnerability keeps each of us open to making the changes we each need to make. We also talk about our career goals and issues we may be having with our children. The other important thing we do in these meetings is tell each other what the other is doing right. We cannot have productive or impactful meetings if we're only focusing on what isn't working. It always amazes me how much effort, focus, and dedication people put into their careers while putting forth very little effort into their love relationships.

Along with the need for us to love others, it's also true that each of us needs love. No one is above or beyond this. Needing love doesn't make us "needy" but normal, healthy human beings. Why is it such a horrible thing these days that when we have needs, we feel some sort of shame and label ourselves as needy? Human beings are interdependent beings. We have reciprocal relationships where we contribute to each other to the best of our abilities.

Let's bottom-line this. For us to not only *be* successful but *feel* successful, we need our love-supports in place. Success has more meaning and feeling when it is a shared part of love. Our emotional supports act as our mirrors, reflecting back to us that we are lovable and doing well and that we are someone to be proud of. And yes, we all need this. Why? It stimulates our motivation and it feels good—something we deserve to feel. When we feel the comforts of those who love and support us, we can be alone and not feel lonely.

Further, feelings of love can come from many different sources. For example, we get love from our pets, our religious or spiritual beliefs, our careers, our relationships, and even our hobbies. But the most important place we need to feel loved is within ourselves, with that love coming from ourselves. Self-love is good and important.

When we have love in our life, we are equipped with that indescribable feeling of connection that helps to carry us through. We have somewhere and someone to whom we belong. Living in this kind of security greatly decreases stress. It's a wonderful feeling knowing we do not have to take on all of life's responsibilities alone. When we're lonely, life feels heavy and unbearable. It makes staying motivated and focused arduous and draining. So let's just humble ourselves to the fact that we all need to love and be loved. There should be no shame in needing this. We are all human after all.

Coachable Moment

Let us always meet each other with a smile,
for the smile is the beginning of love.
—*Mother Teresa*

Love Yourself

Though it may seem counterintuitive, having a strong emotional support system actually better enables you to cope with problems on your own by improving your self-esteem and sense of autonomy. You must see yourself and treat yourself as your most important commodity. In other words, to succeed on any level, you must love yourself. The more you love yourself, the more equipped you are to love others and to allow others to love you.

To love ourselves, we have to go inside and nurture who we are. Because most of us have largely been conditioned to only value loving others, we may feel a sense of guilt or selfishness at the thought of loving ourselves. We may even fear that if we give ourselves too much attention, we'll become self-indulgent. If we give ourselves too much love, we may become narcissistic. Let me make something very clear: Narcissists don't love anyone, including themselves. They are solely about power, control, taking, and manipulation. They are not about loving or giving.

Coachable Moment

You can search throughout the entire universe for someone who is more deserving of your love and affection than you are yourself, and that person is not to be found anywhere. You yourself, as much as anybody in the entire universe, deserves your love and affection.
—*Gautama Buddha*

We all live with ourselves, so isn't it in our best interest to love ourselves? This seems logical to me.

To be emotionally healthy, the best and most lucrative investment we can make is becoming a person we care deeply for. The love we have for ourselves is truly the only love we have any direct control over. So why not make our life easier by loving ourselves and adding our own joy to life's mix? Life in all it colors cannot be enjoyed to the fullest if we haven't the joy from within to capture it. When we cultivate joy from within, it makes our bad days better. On the days where we may feel no one is celebrating us, we know how to celebrate ourselves, or when we don't receive the acknowledgement we deserve, we can provide it for ourselves. When we love ourselves, we take the pressure off of others to keep ourselves going.

I crave my alone time. I have learned that I am never *by* myself; rather, I am *with* myself. Truly loving who I am took time, effort, focus, and a tremendous amount of self-compassion. The moment I started loving myself, I started loving my life, and my life began loving me back. The things I desired to feel and experience were gifted to me much more quickly once I found the love I needed within me. The more content I am in my own self, the easier I am for others to love because there isn't much I need to demand from another to give to me. We must learn to love others under the following agreement: *I will take care of me for you, and I expect you to take care of you for me.* When we approach life this way, we are much easier to love.

As I consider my own life and the lives of all of those with whom I work, I find that the greatest human affliction is a person not feeling good enough about their self. A lack of self-love absolutely affects us, but the good news is there are many ways to work on this. What you have to keep in mind is this: You deserve happiness and the levels of success you desire. So learn to direct your mind-set toward thoughts and feelings that serve your higher good. I ask people to create a check-in list for how well they're doing in loving themselves. When you feel badly about yourself, most of the time it is easy to pinpoint why. It is usually because you're eating poorly, drinking too much, not working out, not getting enough sleep, being lazy, or not managing your thoughts about yourself or others. Make a list of the things that make you feel good and look good so you have the confidence to do better.

Coachable Moment

I have an everyday religion that works for me. Love yourself first, and everything else falls into line.

—Lucille Ball

Success and Love

When we are loved and feel secure in our personal lives, we operate in our business worlds with more confidence. Love makes us confident, and this confidence is extremely important in every aspect of our lives. When we're loved and self-loving, we truly have the power to change the lives of all those we touch. We have the power to leave people feeling better than when they came to us. Nothing makes us more passionate, inspired, or concentrated in our lives or careers than love.

To be successful, we must have the craving, inspiration, and intensity necessary to propel us up the ladder of success. We must desire to move forward. Isn't desire just another form of love? Whether we feel desire for our partner, our business, or our team, desire moves us. Desire keeps us alive and gives us an exciting reason to activate our passions and self-expression in this world. Desire is also undeniably linked to our *purpose.* When we feel a deep love and desire for something, we are inspired. We don't struggle to find motivation nor do we spend time fighting against procrastination. We are ready to go.

If we didn't experience love, nothing of value in this world would even exist. Because desire and inspiration come from love, we have the intensity necessary to create something and to be individuals of great significance. Intensity is necessary to sustain us on our journey. There is no feeling quite as beautiful as that of organic intensity. When we have this, there is nothing that can steal our focus or commitment from the moment we're in. When we work from desire, our success has the potential to be sustaining. True love transcends the basic human tendency toward only wanting to be financially and materially abundant in favor of being truly devoted to who we are, what we do, and what we are capable of offering to others. This is why money alone cannot uphold our happiness in the long-term. We need our soul mates, teammates, spiritual teachers, and coaches for our career to be a genuine reflection of who we are as unique individuals.

Coachable Moment (from my coach)

As every great athlete has a coach, every workplace warrior would do well to have his too. You're leading the charge, you're battling the frontlines. Who's your armor-bearer? Who's got your back?

—*Dr. Dave White*

When we are in healthy, loving relationships, we are more positive, more capable, and more successful. We have people who have our back. We have an advantage because the important parts of our lives are working in harmony. We are not feeling as if we have to shortchange our passions to maintain our relationships. Nor do we have the stress and pressure of our relationships being so destructive to us mentally and emotionally that we are too distracted by them to be effective at work. For us to work to our highest potential, our emotional and business lives must balance and complement each other. There is nothing greater than feeling fully supported in our lives to be whole and to live to do our best.

What is it like to live life with financial gain but have nothing in our hearts? It's not a life at all. It's loneliness. Wealthy is an experience of the heart. Rich is the experience of money. Why not live to have both?

Love in the Workplace

When I mention love in the workplace, I am not talking about having affairs. What I am talking about is showing up and being a really good human being. Love is at the foundation of all empowered and successful relationships. And the most important love attribute you should bring into your work environment is kind-heartedness. It hardly takes an ounce of real effort or time to dramatically change another person's day, including your own. We must look for ways to positively influence and contribute to the people and the environment we are in. We must make it our intention to show up with a positive and uplifting outlook. We should dole out little acts of kind-heartedness and stand in witness of what a huge difference they make in the lives of our family members, friends, employees, colleagues, strangers, and even our own lives.

Successful relationships are reciprocal and based in mutual sharing. Life and work are not all about you. To be known and to deeply know others, we must be willing to share who we are. When we share our thoughts, feelings, and ideas with the intention of taking other people's thoughts and emotions into consideration, it shows we are coming from a place of reciprocity. Reciprocity breeds interest rather than repulsion. When we are reciprocal and open in our approach to communication, people want to hear what we have to say. Effective communication is designed to flow from human to human, on a horizontal level, not from authority figure to subordinate, on a vertical level. A sense of authority may make us feel right or better than others, but when we are reciprocal it makes everyone feel right, pulling us into deep connection with others. Success, of any kind, involves a *coming together* of hearts and minds.

Moreover, it is an act of courage when we show we are never below owning our own foibles and that we are mature enough to apologize whenever necessary. We are all products of our mistakes and what we've learned from them. If we cannot admit wrong, we will not find sustaining success.

In fact, all of us, including you, are going to make mistakes. Knowing this, we must conclude that we will do things that will require an apology from us. Whether you have used your words or actions harmfully or you have omitted information that came out anyway and really hurt someone, you owe it to yourself and others to say, "I am sorry." When you can acknowledge your mistakes and can say any of the following simple three-word statements, "I am sorry," "I was wrong," or "You are right," you start to heal what was broken and to make the necessary changes to rebuild trust wherever necessary. I have never seen anyone choke and die when speaking the words contained in these simple three-word statements. And yet I have seen defensive words destroy others emotionally and lead to severing ties between people. Every apology or statement of ownership brings with it the opportunity for a fresh start.

If we don't know what to do in a situation, we must keep in mind that love is about sharing, so we can ask for advice. When we ask to be shown what to do, we implicitly show respect to the person from whom we are seeking advice. We show that we trust their experience, skill, knowledge, and insight and that we value their opinion. There may be times we need more than input from others. We must show we are open to that by allowing ourselves to be further coached, advised, and trained. Furthermore, whenever we ask for advice in the workplace, we automatically create a reciprocal relationship. To reach the levels of happiness and success we desire, we must humble ourselves to the understanding that advice is temporary but knowledge is forever.

However, leading from reciprocity doesn't equate to being a people-pleaser. Kindness doesn't tolerate disrespect. When we're operating from kindness in the work environment, we have the ability to handle the positive and negative with maturity and grace. On the other hand, insecurity is what leads to tolerating disrespect, which is not an act of kindness. If we desire to be remarkable, we must become well liked and well respected people. Yet this doesn't begin with people-pleasing but with self-assurance. We understand who we are, what we are about, where we are headed, and why we are going in that direction rather than in another. From such a strong foundation, we can listen to others and admit when we are wrong. Likewise, we can let people know when they have crossed a line.

I realize how easy it is to feel terrified or stupid when we're wrong. We may even falsely assume others may lose respect for us if we admit our errors. What I have found, however, is that when we are able to humble ourselves, the respect others have for us actually increases. Our admission of mistakes made tells people everything they need to know about us. It shows them how real we are. And it makes it easier for others to receive correction from us when we find they need it.

No matter who you are or what your title is, you are not immune to being wrong. No one is. Exceptional people understand that being wrong is one of the greatest lessons of all. It is often through being wrong that you learn what not to do. Further, the painful experience of being wrong allows others the same courtesy in your life. Being wrong joins us all to being one-in-the-same. Believe it or not, when you come off as perfect, people experience you to be less approachable, more intimidating, and unkind. When people see your success, along with your natural flaws, you are experienced as more approachable, kind, empathetic, and flexible. The more approachable you are to others, the more successful your relationships will be.

Kindness and humility are markers of exceptional character. People want to work with humble people. And when we're humble, we are comfortable acknowledging others and their contributions. In reality, we can never give too much praise. Having a positive impact on others is simple. Tell them where they shine, how they contribute, and why they matter. When we feel appreciated and express our appreciation for others, we increase their motivation to work that much harder. It's nearly impossible to work from a place of feeling underappreciated. After all, if our hard work and results don't matter, what is our motivation to continue? We must never forget what others do for us in our lives. Acknowledgment is the greatest and most heartfelt form of payment.

So be loving to people. Become a lover of humans. That's my hashtag: #loverofhumans. Life is so much easier when we are people loving.

And yes, we can be loving at work too. We can show our kindness, loyalty, and support to our colleagues through cooperation, listening, and being available. It is impossible to lose any ground or status when being kind to people. Results come and go in life and business, but feelings are forever. If we publicly criticize employees, it may seem they eventually get over it, but inside they never do. Impeccable self-management skills are necessary to the development of positive connections. Living in a world that has largely become self-centered, mean, egotistical, and greedy, we each must seize the opportunity to *Be The Difference.* We must strive to live on the side of caring deeply about the well-being, happiness, and success of others.

Why not make it a daily decision to bring positive love-energy into every environment you're in? I wholeheartedly believe kindness will take you further in life than any other human characteristic. You cannot protect others or yourself from all of life's tragedies, but you can allow yourself to surround and be surrounded by those whom you love and support and who love and support you in return. You accomplish this through kindness. Give your time, love, and attention to those who need it. When love is at the basis of your relationships, reciprocity is present. You will seldom feel lonely or lost—no matter how challenging things may be. When you're loved, you live from a deep sense of security that makes it possible to take risks and to accept defeats.

Coachable Moment
Life in abundance comes only through great love.
—*Elbert Hubbard*

Toxic Love

Our society is more health conscious than ever before. We are paying increased attention to nutrition labels, fitness opportunities, organic foods, toxin-free environments, and more. And yet, we who are health conscious often don't realize that the quality of our relationships can be just as toxic to our health as fast food or a bad environment. In fact, unhealthy relationships can turn into a toxic internal environment that will undoubtedly and quickly lead us into stress, depression, anxiety, distractibility, and even medical problems. Toxic relationships can occur between partners, friends, parents and children, and coworkers, to name just a few situations. No relationship, of course, is blissful and conflict-free, but *difficult* and *toxic* ones are markedly different.

There is a great deal of information available about love and how to make love work. Love brings us hope and purpose. We hope our bosses and colleagues approve of us, we hope our friends see the good in us, and we hope we can find lasting love with a partner who sustains and empowers us. Still, too many of us love those who aren't loving us in return. Hope is the emotion largely responsible for keeping us locked in, trying to fit a square peg in a round hole. When our personal life is negative, it has the power to completely short circuit our ability to be functional anywhere else, especially at work.

Here are some ideas to clarify when a relationship is toxic and not good for your life or career.

Healthy relationships are clear, not confusing

If there is a clear indicator that we're in a healthy relationship or not, it is our answer to this question: *Is my relationship clear or confusing?* The more confusing a relationship is, the more we have to guess about where we stand and the more we feel as if we're walking on eggshells. These are just some of the signs of an unhealthy relationship. Such relationships create stress in our lives. And the more stress we feel, the more debilitated we become in our ability to think clearly and work efficiently because we're constantly distracted by the toxic persons in our lives. Our mind becomes consumed with worry and our bodies flooded with adrenaline. Our blood pressure runs high from the fears we harbor as we wonder when the other shoe is going to unexpectedly drop. This type of worry pulls us away from work. Our body may be present, but our mind is not.

Healthy relationships experience disagreement, not fighting

When a relationship is healthy, occasional differences of opinion are expected and discussed without either person feeling disrespected, unheard, or ill treated in any other way. People in healthy relationships actually expect their partners to be different from them. And the differences are usually appreciated.

When the relationship is unhealthy, disagreements escalate into full-blown arguments, even shouting matches, or horrible silent treatments until the more passive partner succumbs to the control of the more dominant one. We lose self-respect and so much more in these toxic dynamics. This is tragic and unnecessary. When we don't respect ourselves, others sense it, stop respecting us, and come to view us as emotionally unbalanced, which is not the reputation we want, especially at work.

Healthy love is relationship oriented, not agenda oriented

It's often hard to tell the difference between love and manipulation, which is why many of us end up loving manipulators, falsely believing that the way life is with them is normal.

Healthy relationships are not invested in asserting control or power over partners. Such relationships are truly open and flexible.

Unhealthy relationships are largely skewed toward meeting the needs of only one person. In this dynamic, one person's idea of the relationship is based on measuring how much the other person is willing to do for them. Don't think manipulators stop manipulating just because we go to work. When we have to answer more calls from our partner than emails or texts to our boss, or vice versa, we have a problem.

Healthy relationships are honest, not hypocritical

When relationships are healthy, the people in them possess the integrity to be honest with each other, even when it hurts. Empathy is present where active listening occurs and defenses are down so feedback can be received and given with a level of mutual respect and understanding. When we feel supported in our private lives, we have the tools to better communicate in the work environment.

Unhealthy relationships function around rules one person rigidly places upon others, but this person does not live by the rules he or she applies to others. Whenever the unfair person is confronted, he or she becomes immediately defensive, deflects, and projects all the problems, in a circular fashion, back onto others. This type of stress forces us to put our career to the side to manage what is happening in the relationship causing us stress. When we are emotionally consumed and off-balance, people experience us as negative, easily distracted, and unable to carry our workload.

Healthy relationships are positive, not negative

Healthy love is fun, easy, joyful, relaxed, and quiet. Each person knows it's their choice what type of emotion, attitude, and effort they bring into the relational dynamic. In healthy relationships, each person makes a conscious choice to focus on the positive qualities of other individuals. When we're happy, we approach life ready, focused, and prepared to give our all to whatever and whomever is in front of us.

Unhealthy relationships focus solely on the negative qualities of others. They are run by criticism, sarcasm, manipulation, and passive aggression. Each time an infraction occurs, it creates a nuclear war. How effective can we function in this type of dynamic?

Healthy relationships are free, not controlled

For healthy relationships to exist, there has to be space for each partner to think rationally about the relationship. Healthy relationship dynamics allow each person the necessary rope to have a life outside the relationship, to do the things each needs to do to be independently happy, healthy, and successful. These types of relationships allow and encourage the success of the other.

Unhealthy relationships are socially isolated. They tend to be controlled, usually by one person whose insecurities squash the independence of the other. When any relationship dominates our time and energy, we end up unable to function in other important areas of our lives.

Healthy relationships compliment, don't put down

Healthy relationship dynamics are empowering. Each person is proud and supportive of the other, and this is acknowledged verbally and emotionally. Healthy relationships are communicative, encouraging, and nurturing. Each person is empowered to live his or her dreams and to get up and keep going after any type of personal failure. We work better when we're supported to be at our best.

Unhealthy dynamics, however, neither enjoy nor celebrate the independence or success of the other person and seem to relish when the other person experiences failure, which is often backed with an "I told you so." These dynamics are draining. They decrease motivation to perform because we come to believe nothing we do is ever enough or ever good enough.

Healthy relationships aren't nitpicky but find the humor

Healthy relationship dynamics allow for human error. There are always going to be things about people that annoy us a little or even a lot, but in healthy dynamics these idiosyncrasies are seen as human and acceptable. When we feel accepted, we have an increased sense of confidence to perform because we're allowed to make mistakes and learn.

Unhealthy relationships sweat the small stuff so intensely that if one person, for example, is ten minutes late, it can literally ruin the entire day for the other. These relationships focus on rigid rules as the determiners of importance and respect, which keeps the relationship in total distress over issues that just don't matter. When we are treated this way, we live in a constant state of anxiety, which inevitably leaks into our work life, causing us to be extremely sidetracked and off balance.

Healthy love is intimate, not resentful

In speaking about intimacy, I'm not referring to the workplace but to the home. Being sexually loved at home is incredibly important for our success at work. Healthy relationships are fun, open, and intimate. When two people love and respect each other, intimacy is their playground. These couples cuddle, hold hands, kiss, and express other forms of intimacy on a regular basis.

Unhealthy "love" is so consumed with broken rules, no-win games, and conflict that the couples in such relationships don't like each other enough to want intimacy.

The more sexually happy and satisfied we are, the more fulfilled we are and the better we perform in all areas of our lives.

Healthy relationship dynamics are possible. They are shared between people who are willing to consciously contribute to every aspect of the dynamic to make sure what they share is authentically loving and healthy. Each partner is supported to live their individual life to the fullest. When we are loved, respected, and confident in our love relationships, we go to work at ease, we make fewer mistakes, and we are more social and well liked by our colleagues. Anything less than this type of healthy dynamic becomes stressful.

⊰⎯⎯⎯

Coachable Moment
A healthy relationship is one in which
love enriches you, not imprisons you.
—*Steve Maraboli*

⎯⎯⎯⊱

Healthy Boundaries

Love + HEALHTY BOUNDARIES = Emotional Security

Boundaries are the edges that should exist between ourselves and other people. They are the limits that say, *This is where I stop and you start.* When we have an idea of limits, it allows us to live healthier lives and to be healthier in our relationships. When we are dealing with toxic relationships, we have to learn to set limits so we don't lose ourselves. Boundaries communicate that we have self-value.

How can we reach our desired levels of success when we have negative people hanging from our lives like lead balls? We cannot be effective when drama clutters and weighs down our lives. It only takes one toxic person to completely destroy your life and the lives of many others. There is no path to healthy self-love if you do not have the healthy limits in place to protect yourself. You must get clear on what you deserve and what you're unwilling to tolerate.

Once your boundaries are in place, your life will shift. It will open up in ways you could have never imagined. Positive relationships are an important part of the formula for a healthy, successful, and well-balanced life. You must make sure that your health-conscious lifestyle doesn't leave out this crucial ingredient.

Devastating Consequences of Unhealthy Boundaries

Unhealthy boundaries come from fear we project onto others. This fear is based in our past experience with overtly controlling and manipulative people. If we approach our lives from fear, we likely developed this habit from our childhood.

When we are fearful, we find it harder to set boundaries because we are people wary, causing us to mistakenly use people pleasing as a way to cope. We may feel as if it is nearly impossible to say no due to our anxiety over being rejected or facing anger or abandonment. This anxiety causes us to go against ourselves and our own needs in favor of meeting the needs of others. We do this believing it will make us emotionally safe, but this couldn't be further from the truth. Without healthy limits and boundaries in place, we have no protection at all. This self-destructive habit has the tragic effect of leading us away from establishing a necessary balance of power and responsibility in our relationships. Instead we lean toward being overly responsible, passive, and dependent, and we take on other people's problems as our own.

Another misstep we make out of the desire to be accepted is to share personal information about ourselves with others far before we have established any real trust or connection with them. Unfortunately, when we share too much too soon with a toxic person, what we share is almost always used later for our exploitation. When our self-worth is low, we allow ourselves to be too tolerant to the abuse and disrespect of others, causing us to further lose our confidence. We lose track of our own inner compass, allowing who we are, our potential included, to be determined by others. This makes us completely dependent on the ideas, values, and opinions of those outside of us. We mistakenly compromise what we believe in because we're afraid to face conflict. When we have poor boundaries, we get in our own way of succeeding, growing, and living authentically.

The Elevating Payoffs of Healthy Boundaries

We must have healthy boundaries and a healthy sense of ourselves to be successful. We must start practicing saying yes or no when we need to and also accept when others say yes or no to us. When we set healthy limits around ourselves, we feel an inner power and freedom to be exactly who we are and to give that same grace to others.

To set healthy boundaries, we must have a strong identity. And to establish a strong identity, we need to start setting healthy boundaries. We must respect ourselves wholly and refuse to tolerate abuse or disrespect of any kind. We all deserve this.

Coaching Moment

Truly powerful people don't explain why they want respect. They simply don't engage someone who doesn't give it to them.

—Sherry Argov

When we are strong in who we are, we are mindful to only involve ourselves in relationships that are mutually beneficial. We know our wants, needs, and feelings and are able to communicate them clearly with others. We stand committed to and responsible for exploring and nurturing ourselves to reach our full potential. We consider ourselves as being solely responsible for our own feelings of happiness and fulfillment. We communicate our personal limits and appreciate and respect the limits of others. We choose to lead our lives from empathy and are wise to wait before becoming too self-revealing in our relationships. We wait for trust to be established. Most importantly, we are never above asking for help when we need it, and we do not compromise on our values or integrity just to avoid rejection.

I realize that setting limits takes a tremendous amount of courage, but the more you do it, the easier it gets and the healthier life you will lead. How wonderful would it be to live the miracles you dream of? When you have the necessary limits in place, you give yourself the freedom to say no without guilt and to say yes because you want to rather than doing so out of some internalized guilt or sense of obligation. When you honor your limits, you become the owner and keeper of your life. As you get better, I can guarantee that you will never again settle for less.

One of the many gifts that setting boundaries and self-love give you is strength of character. When I set boundaries or coach others to do this, it is done for self-preservation. You have rights, you have worth, and you have value. If you do not stand for those qualities in yourself by setting limits on what you will and will not tolerate, you cannot effectively captain the ship of your own life. Boundaries are a direct way to love and respect yourself.

Success Benefits of Conflict

We must do all we can to become comfortable with conflict. When we are conflict allergic, it is common to become sweaty, our voice may start shaking, and our skin may visibly flush. This is a fight-or-flight response that is designed to protect us, but more often than not it gets in our way. Any time we are placed in a position to say no or to have a different opinion than others, we face the potential of conflict. For this reason, we may as well take some time to examine conflict's benefits.

- *Conflict opens our eyes to new ideas.* As thoughts are expressed back and forth, we allow someone else to fine-tune the truth we are trying to speak as our truth rubs against theirs. In this way conflict is as creative as it is a fine-tuning instrument to your individuality.
- *Conflict forces us to stand up for ourselves.* When we stand up for ourselves, we set our limits and make them clear to others, thereby letting people know who we are with a crisp clarity. Conflict provides us with the opportunity to verbalize our needs and get them met.
- *Conflict teaches flexibility.* If we are in conflict, we are not just going to have others adjust to us and our truth, but we will also be adjusting to someone else and their truth. Out of conflict can come healthy compromise.
- *Conflict teaches us to listen.* The key to any successful conflict is learning to listen. Listening must be active, not passive, and listening requires self-control. We need to make it our goal not to remain quiet until the other person is done talking.
- *Conflict teaches us patterns of behavior.* As we engage in conflict, we will learn how others think, their style of communication, and their points of view. Knowing patterns helps us become more effective in our relationships because patterns provide us with forms of predictability. We learn to more readily tell what someone will say or how they will respond to us and others.
- *Conflict leads to solutions.* When what was isn't working any longer, something new has to be formed to establish a new relationship or a new way for things to operate. In some way, conflict is a form of brainstorming with the end result being a new solution or a new path.
- *Conflict provides an opportunity to practice communicating.* The more we engage in conflict, the better of a communicator we will become. I'm not urging you to go out and create conflicts. Instead I want you

to be unafraid to participate in conflict when it arises. Treat it as an opportunity to better formulate what you want to say and how you want others to understand you.

- *Conflict is an opportunity to set limits.* As we set and experience our limits, we are learning a good deal about ourselves that we can now communicate. We can learn to either back off, or we can learn to activate for ourselves and ask someone else to step back.

- *Conflict provides an opportunity to practice emotional self-control.* We do not have to be so emotional all the time. If we want to be taken seriously, we must approach conflict judiciously. We must learn to remain calm, to say the least amount of words to get our point across, and to stay firm in setting our way.

- *Conflict provides an opportunity for us to differentiate ourselves from other people.* We can learn a great deal about who we are through the differences we have with other people and the way life often works. This is called differentiation. Differentiation is our capacity to tell our truth as clearly as we see it all the while remaining engaged with those who are different from us.

Conflict provides us with the opportunity to put a true representation of ourselves out in the world. Speaking the truth about ourselves in the midst of disagreement is the foundation of emotional health. When we can speak the truth about who we are, it allows everything in the conversation to absorb and respond to that information which creates an adjustment in the other. In that instant, you have made a positive change.

Coachable Moment
Conflict doesn't require agreement. It requires adjustment.
—Sherrie Campbell

Emotional Security
Love + Healthy Boundaries = EMOTIONAL SECURITY

Healthy, intimate, trusting, successful relationships are built on a foundation of emotional safety. Knowing we are in relationships with people who have our best interest at heart gives us a sense of comfort. We can trust that we will remain a priority to them through the unexpected twists and turns life brings. These significant relationships provide us with a safe place to fall. We all need our loves and supports to buffer us from life's sharper edges. Unconditional love does wonders for our confidence and motivation to get up and continue trying. To live fearing that the bottom is going to fall out at an unexpected time is a terrible way to go through life. We cannot achieve sustaining success from this type of anxiety. Success of any type comes from choosing trustworthy people to uphold us. With these types of relationships, we are invincible.

We all need three key ingredients when giving or receiving love: the experience of feeling heard, loved, and understood. When these key ingredients are present and consistent, relationships flourish. Here's a rule of thumb I give my clients: *Follow through on your promises, keep your word, and demonstrate your love and support in a reliable fashion.* If you engage others this way, you will show love and honor to them as well as to yourself. You will more regularly experience feeling heard, loved, and understood.

To nurture and promote our relationships, our business, and our personal lives, we must be emotionally engaged and available. We must have the courage and integrity to make our needs known to others through the mutual sharing of ideas, values, opinions, and fears. We must be receptive to hearing people out to continue moving forward. When communication is straight and honest, emotional security is the result. When we share these elements with our lovers, friends, bosses, and children, our relationships have a sense of predictability and consistency.

It's virtually a truism that as we become increasingly successful, we take on more stress and responsibility. We need supports to establish the grit necessary to overcome our challenges. And this is where the combination of love and healthy boundaries comes in. Together they give us the emotional security we need to face the challenges sure to come.

MARINATE ON THIS

There are realities we all share, regardless of our nationality, language, or individual tastes. As we need food, so do we need emotional nourishment: love, kindness, appreciation, and support from others. We need to understand our environment and our relationship to it. We need to fulfill certain inner hungers: the need for happiness, for peace of mind, for wisdom.

—J. Donald Walters

Failure + Persistence = Overcoming

The first step to building resilience is to take responsibility for who you are and for your life. If you're not willing to do that, stop wasting your time reading this letter. The essence of responsibility is the acceptance of the consequences—good and bad—of your actions.
—Eric Greitens

To overcome and be resilient, we can take nothing for granted. We must take time each day to count our blessings and not allow ourselves to become sidetracked by what we don't have or how far away we are from reaching our goals. We must trust our fearlessness and refuse to allow any one issue to keep us down for too long. We must always be wise to the value of preparation, and be eternally grateful to have a team of emotional supports in place, helping us think through and strategize on our next steps. We must remember to respect the great courage it takes to continue moving forward in our lives when the next steps seem vague and unknown.

Before we continue talking through the success equations, take a moment to embrace, as fully as you can, that feeling of being most alive when you grind hard at or toward something that holds deep meaning for you. We feel the most prosperous and fortunate while in the middle of our journey. We get to see how life works in our favor, even when things look bleak. We bear witness to the inner strength we have when we have needed it most. We have moments when we stand in amazement at ourselves for all we have learned, for the fears we have faced, and what we have been able to accomplish through the simple act of being persistent. Challenge, fear, and even joy are there so we can overcome them.

Overcome joy?

Yes.

Joy is a moment attached to an achievement, and the moment following this joy will be a new and unpredictable moment we must prepare for and learn from. All things pass in a cyclical fashion. We must always be prepared for our next moment, our next challenge, our next potential for joy, for each moment will test our potential to achieve and overcome it.

We must let nothing defeat our efforts.

This is what it means to overcome.

Failure

FAILURE + Persistence = Overcoming

Heartbreak is woven in and out of every crevice of life and business. How we transcend failure and heartbreak is largely determined by how we think and what we push ourselves to do, be, and have while in the throes of it. If used correctly, heartbreak and failure become the springboards to a better life leading to increased success.

Heartbreak is a powerful force. It is here to cleanse our lives of what isn't working, whether we realize that or not. Heartbreak is responsible for our evolution as a person. It teaches us about the interconnectedness of joy and destruction. It teaches us where our holes are. It teaches us what not to do again, who to avoid, and who we need to be to do better going forward.

Heartbreak feels debilitating, and for a time it often is, but neither failure nor heartbreak are the end of you. *You* are not finished yet. Heartbreak is temporary.

It is a momentary passage through time that serves to deepen your capacity to count on yourself, to learn to think on your feet, and to thrive.

Make Peace with Failure

Hardship, failure, and rejection are the pitfalls along any road to success. When we resist these traumas, we work against accepting the lessons being offered within the heartbreak they create.

It's natural to get down on ourselves when things aren't going our way. We too easily fall into the trap of self-blame and self-recrimination, which ends up being more painful and enduring than the failure-event or heartbreak itself. The inner dialogue we have with ourselves can either lead us toward a place of healing or into our own self-destruction. We must hold tight to the idea of acceptance. We must accept and understand the situation we are in, and examine what factors led us to this place. If there was a way in, there is certainly a way out. Acceptance is not a form of giving up; it is a form of opening up. When we accept the reality of our circumstances for what they are, new possibilities and solutions immediately show up. When we fight and resist our circumstances, we spin our wheels but remain stuck.

When we reflect on past failures, we discover similarities in the patterns of our own thoughts and behaviors that contributed to our problem. We also come to understand that there were many elements of our situation beyond our control. When we stop resisting, fighting, and self-abusing, we can differentiate between what was us and came from us and the aspects of our situation that we had no control over. When we see the aspects of our situation we could not have prevented or prepared for, our emotions surrounding the failure and heartbreak naturally ease, helping us to overcome.

Take charge of your life. You are the only person responsible for you, and you are the one person who can get you back on your feet. When you're hurting, make decisions that serve to get you through the hurt.

You cannot remain stagnant and expect personal growth. Take time to process and digest by writing your feelings or talking them out with a trusted person. Failure is your time to dig in and prove something to yourself about yourself.

There is no easy way out of failure or heartbreak. You must do the needed work.

Focus solely on you. Do not compare yourself to others. This type of mind-set is defeatist. When you focus on yourself, you will find the power and resources necessary to dramatically change your vibe, your trajectory, and the overall state of your mind.

Coachable Moment

Someone once asked me, why do you always insist on taking the hard road? I replied, why do you assume I see two roads?
— *"The Idealist"*

Time Heals

Whenever we are in the middle of heartbreak, the great healer is always time and space.

Time is the element of healing we dislike most because we want our feelings of heartbreak to pass through as quickly as possible. In reality, most of us would give nearly anything to have failure hurt less than it does. But failure is what it is, and it hurts.

When failures come—and they certainly will—we need to take them as opportunities to train ourselves to sit in the pocket of pain and uncertainty but with a sense of bravery. As we learn to fully embrace our reality and open our heart to the heartbreak, these painful times will pass more quickly. However, sitting in the pocket of uncertainty and pain does not equate to sit, wait, and wallow. It means to feel, be, do, and have. In my deepest moments of having to traverse through life's pain, which I have had to do a lot, I learned that the most effective way through my pain was to surrender and accept my circumstances. I did not accept my circumstances from a mind-set of defeat but rather because I was completely unable to worry, cry, scream, or yell my circumstances into being different than they were. In my painful times, I had to actively and forcefully move myself toward accepting life on its own terms. In letting down all the resistances I had put up, I surrendered. I allowed myself to fall and to feel vulnerable, weak, and needy. I learned that I had to experience my pain, like it or not, to get rid of it. I journaled about it, I traveled with it, and I got to deeply know it. My pain became my partner, my teacher, and eventually my savior. When I was resisting the pain and fears in my heart, I was fighting with them rather than growing from them. When I accepted my pain, my pain accepted me too. In the process, I found that my pain was not bottomless and without solution. I found it was full of lessons and opportunities. Although I have never enjoyed any of my journeys through suffering, I have become a better person because of them.

Recovery of any sort is the healthiest when it is an active recovery, not a complete halt of movement. Effectively dealing with heartbreak is a full-time job.

It's also true that heartbreak, in essence, is the backdoor to success. Every successful person will tell you they have failed way more than they have ever succeeded and that it was their failures that made them into who they are today. Heartbreak molds, defines, and evolves our character. So embrace heartbreak. Open your mind and heart to its teachings. The positive thing about challenging times is they stretch your capacity to feel bad and fail while evolving your capacity to feel joy and succeed.

Success is a climb. It's a journey. It's lifelong and designed around undulating and unpredictable ups and downs. Success is always built on risk, change, and personal development. The journey teaches us to cope with failure. Fundamental to the teachings of success is to get up and push onward toward our dreams, regardless of the obstacles we face. Many of us start our journey with pie-in-the-sky, smooth-road ideals. Yet success is rarely, if ever, that type of journey. It is usually easy to start. The question is, will we finish? We have to have a *made-up mind* to go all the way, not halfway or three-quarters of the way. We must believe that we are designed to finish.

We cannot allow anything to get in the way of us fulfilling our unique assignment in this world. We cannot stay bitter and discouraged and still become the person we were created to be. If we want to succeed, we must have the resilience to face the inevitable and overcome.

☀️

Coachable Moment

I've missed more than 9000 shots in my career. I've lost almost 300 games. 26 times, I've been trusted to take the game winning shot and missed. I've failed over and over and over again in my life. And that is why I succeed.

—Michael Jordan

On this journey we are going to feel pain. This is true for every successful person, so we're not alone. In fact, we're actually among the elite. Suffering is an integral and essential part of any real pursuit of success. Nothing about success comes easy, but every painful story has the potential to have a triumphant ending. We must let this knowledge inspire us. We must desire victory after defeat. We are all capable. We must train ourselves to see each day as a day that we are blessed with new chances and opportunities to start from the place we find ourselves. Uncertainty and struggle are inevitable; yet, both prompt us to make adjustments to mitigate their effects, mentoring us toward success.

The People Problem

It is also all too common that as we reach further and further into our own success, we lose relationships. As sad as this feels, it is true. As we get closer to the top, we'll find fewer people traveling with us. We'll discover that some who came with us earlier will stop supporting us, causing us much confusion and heartbreak. Success takes a tremendous amount of effort and sacrifice. The effort and time we need to put into our journey will be intolerable to some who feel we owe them more of our time, effort, or energy. To be successful, we will need to sacrifice an enormous amount to get to where we want to go. This doesn't mean we abandon all other things but that we have to understand that not all others will approve of or understand our quest. We must trust that the people meant to take this journey with us will accept and support the sacrifices we need to make. We will likely lose those other relationships with people who do not passionately share in our vision.

Another reason some people problems will arise is jealousy. Jealousy is a deadly emotion for many. They cannot see their own dreams clearly enough to support ours. These people will do all they can to discourage us and tell us that our priorities are our-of-whack, and the beliefs we hold about what we want to achieve are selfish and unrealistic. Let them keep their opinions. They have nothing to do with you.

We, due to all the gossip and chatter, will undoubtedly go through periods where it will be difficult not to question ourselves based on the negative opinions of others. Nine times out of ten when we start a new venture, we will go in and out of feeling utterly paralyzed. When we know we're being mocked or doubted by others, it's easy to doubt ourselves. Sometimes we may doubt our knowledge and the decisions we've already made. We may even come to doubt our own instincts. All of this doubt creates an internal conflict over what we need to do to move forward. We don't want to make the wrong decisions and end up in what we fear will be an unrecoverable mistake.

The good news is that there are no unrecoverable mistakes! There are only new directions.

We must push through our doubts and not allow them to partner up with delay. Doubt and delay, when paired, derail success.

Don't let doubt stifle you. Don't let it freeze you out of options. Realize that a certain amount of self-doubt can be incredibly motivating. It is amazing what we'll do to avoid failure, to have the opportunity to prove all the naysayers and petty bullies wrong. Doubts are an inevitable part of succeeding. The important thing is that we continue to stay in action in spite of them.

Coachable Moment

What others say and do is a projection of their own reality, their own dream. When you are immune to the opinions and actions of others, you won't be the victim of needless suffering.

—*Don Miguel Ruiz*

I advise that keep your dreams close to your chest. When you share them, you risk pillaging them to dream-stealers and naysayers. The human mind is programmed to believe the negative. When you set out on the road less traveled, you will have an audience full of small-minded people trying to scare you and discourage you from chasing your dreams. These are the people who want to instill so much fear in you that you stay living as the smaller version of yourself they are most comfortable with. But part of your personal growth is to make yourself immune to these influences. So work quietly and allow your success to do the talking.

When I was studying for my state boards, I told no one. I didn't need anyone else digging into how I was studying, what prep course I chose, and what practice test scores I was getting. All of this chatter would have pulled me from my focus and put me into comparison with others, what they were doing, and the scores they were getting. I kept all of this to myself. Consequently I crushed that test while many of the smarter but more vocal doctoral students failed it. I passed because I didn't engage in any posturing or game playing. It was my test to take, not a competition I was in with others. Also, if I had failed that test, I wouldn't have needed to advertise it or do the walk of shame in front of those I had been bragging to. Keep your ego in check and your dreams to yourself.

As people begin to witness us live our dreams, their jealousy can quickly turn to hatred. Many people don't tend to like other successful people. A jealousy can come along with being different, standing out, and chasing our dreams. Small people detest those who have or do everything they will not.

Dealing with jealousy can be difficult, especially when we want to maintain our relationships with certain people. According to the psychology of violence, jealousy is the most violent of all the emotions because people seek to destroy what they envy. If any around us become hateful, we may need to let them go.

In reality, there will always be a certain percentage of people who will not like us no matter who we are or what we do. We can make use of these people and our experiences with them to toughen up our mental fitness. Most importantly, we should use them to fuel our drive. Your success is the best way to suddenly play your ace.

Coachable Moment
Let your haters make you greater.
—*Steve Harvey*

Doubt and Hope

When in the chase for your dreams, replace doubt with hope. We must let the magical quality of hope act as our dope. Hope keeps us dreaming and believing. The rewards of what we achieve can be great, as can the cost.

Failure helps cultivate the virtue of overcoming, which we will need for our long-term success. Failure's purpose is to fine-tune our efforts toward achieving our dreams. One thing that is guaranteed: *it will all be worth it.* To achieve anything, we have to think positively about what we are doing. We have to believe, down to every cell in our body, that what we are doing is right.

With the right ideas, attitudes, and thoughts, the things you struggle with are nothing but another part of your process. It all starts with you. When you fall in love with a great idea, fate will push you to follow that path. When you see that your success improves and positively impacts the lives of others, you will see your effort as worth the price you paid. I don't believe "destination" to be a place. I believe destination is an emotional experience—the experience of what it feels like to deeply move, help, and contribute to the world at large. That type of destination makes the struggle of the journey well worth it.

Know When to Let Go

Loss and change are going to happen whether we like it or not. We will be forced to learn to let go as a part of our process of moving ahead. Look at it this way: if we never had to let go, we would never learn how to move on. The steadfast ability to move on is one of the greatest powers to cultivate as an integral and necessary part of our character. It takes tremendous will to move on. Therefore, we must know when to let go and to not confuse letting go with giving up.

Giving up is quitting, while letting go is wisdom.

Letting go is perhaps one of the hardest things we do in life. When we lose something that we loved and wanted with all of our heart, we go through a grieving process that we must traverse before becoming rational again in our thinking. Letting go is often the only way back to regaining clarity in a mind that wants to continue holding on. Letting go is not for the weak. It is for those willing to face losses that many others cannot.

It is through letting go that we discover the strength of our will, the pliability of our spirits, and the strength of our personal greatness. While all of this is good, letting go is still hard to do and this is so for several reasons.

Letting go is maddening

It's excruciating to force ourselves to let go of something we invested our time, energy, love, and effort into, especially when we were deeply convinced that our investment was 100 percent worth it. Letting go teaches us that what we had originally thought was so incredible, maybe wasn't as fantastic as we had hoped. Life, over time, forces us to let go of the things that are out of balance, even if we cannot see this at the time. If something breaks, it is usually because it was already weak, prone to becoming broken.

It's a maddening process to fight the treacherous eight-inch distance between the mind and the heart. The mind moves quickly forward as the heart seeks desperately to hang on. But this is the process we must engage in until we become clear and have regained a state of mental and emotional balance.

Letting go is intelligent

Letting go speaks highly to having the humility to accept life on its terms. This is not easy to do. Yet, when we hang on, we suffer. When we hang on, we lose all contact with our ability to think clearly because our emotions are consistently working to derail us. The more we grasp and hold on, the more stuck and desperate we feel.

The wise thing to do when life is creating drastic changes without your consent is to work on trusting that if something is leaving your life, it must not have been meant to be a significant part of your future. This is not something you come to believe in an instant. Rather you come to this belief through practicing faith and surrender.

Letting go is courageous

It takes tremendous faith to surrender to a process that our mind and emotions are fighting. We must be brave in face of uncertainty, knowing it takes much mental effort to keep ourselves upright on the road less traveled. If we clutch to something, we may feel good and secure in the moment, but in the end we will not move onto the bigger and better things waiting for us. And there *are* bigger and better things.

The most courageous way to know if something is truly meant for us is to let it go. If it is meant for us, the opportunity will return. Courage always involves risk. When there is no other choice, we must *drop it, leave it, and let it go.*

During my doctoral program, I made a critical and painful mistake. I was unaware or somehow missed that I needed a specific document signed from my school for the Board of Psychology prior to starting my fifteen hundred pre-doctoral residency hours. I had completed these hours unaware that anything was missing. When I submitted them to the Board of Psychology for approval, they were rejected. It did not matter that every single residency hour I had accumulated had been documented and signed off by a supervisor. I lost all fifteen hundred hours and was told I would have to start over. I was devastated. I felt defeated. I had all the proof to show that I had worked those hours, but the Board of Psychology still refused to accept them.

At first, I tried to fight the board's decision. I was angry with the board and with my school advisor for not making it crystal clear to me what the board needed before I started my pre-doctoral residency work. And I was ashamed of myself. I was so bitter, but none of that changed the situation. I had to accept my situation and take ownership of my oversight. For a long period, each time I would think about this, I would feel angry at my advisor and with the Board of Psychology. But my anger helped nothing. I finally realized that I had to force myself to stop picking up my feelings of bitterness again and again and just move on to find another way up the mountain.

I am happy to say that two miracles came out of this acceptance. The first was that I had more time to myself for about three months before I started working eighty hours a week to accomplish both my pre-doctoral and post-doctoral hours at the same time. During this three-month break, I became pregnant with my daughter. I had been trying to get pregnant for two years and was beginning to worry that maybe it wasn't going to happen for me. The second miracle is that I was accepted into my dream residency—the one I had applied to earlier and didn't get due to open slots already having been filled. When I finally finished all my hours, I was only three months behind where I would have been had I not made my initial mistake. And in the big picture of my life, I was blessed with the pregnancy of the love of my life, my daughter London. Letting my bitterness go provided time and space for new opportunities to come into my life that made all the loss and change worth it. What I learned from this is, if we don't leave our bitterness behind and we continue to pick it up over and over, we place ourselves in a position to carry bitterness or a grudge for years to come. And we may miss out on even greater opportunities and blessings while we focus so relentlessly on nursing our wounds. How much better it is to learn to let it go and move on.

Letting go requires patience

Patience is a painful state of mind to endure. The place of waiting is always trying and horribly difficult to live out because we cannot predict, with any accuracy, how our lives will be impacted from the change we are going through.

Cravings for clarity, stability, and security, when fueled by our fears, cause us to be impulsive. When we act out, we tend to make our situation worse, not better. What we need, then, is to be patient. As hard as it is, patience helps us outlast our preconceptions and anxieties. When we are hurt, afraid, confused, or feeling out of control, we must wait. When we wait, the things we fear, when given the grace of time, fall into place and come to make perfect sense.

Letting go is powerful

It takes far greater courage to let go than it does to clutch and hang on. If we are grasping at something, we are coming from an emotionally out-of-control place, believing that it will be impossible to move on without whatever it was that we lost. The more we grasp at something, however, the more we suffocate it and the greater the likelihood it is that we will lose it.

To really know if something is meant to be in our lives, we must let it go and learn to live without it. We must give ourselves permission to take time away to empower ourselves to better our lives and show ourselves that we can put ourselves first whenever we need to and go on whether or not we have all the things we want.

Letting go is respectful

When a change comes, we have two choices: We can resist the change or we can accept it.

When we resist change, we hurt. We hurt because we want our reality to be different than it is.

When we accept the changes that come, understanding that acceptance is a process. We respect ourselves, we respect life, and we learn to trust that all change is meant for our good.

When we clutch, beg, get bitter, or hang on when we know we need to let go, not only do we lose self-respect but we also lose the respect of our peers, loves, and colleagues.

It takes great composure to let go in a way where we still maintain our dignity. When we meet adversity with dignity, we make others wonder if taking an opportunity from us will end up as *their* mistake.

Letting go brings closure

Whenever we let go of something—such as a job, a deal, a financial loss, an important business relationship, or a love relationship—there is an unsettling, grieving process that accompanies it. The movie *Jerry Maguire* is a great example of how closing one door serves to open another one. In that movie, Jerry's old firm fires him from the company he helped build. This was an emotional death for Jerry. In one moment of honesty, he lost everything he knew. The grief he experienced in trying to find himself was profound. The losses he experienced put him directly, and not so gently, on the journey for the deeper meaning in life he was searching for but wasn't finding in his old life. The loss of his financial empire left him with little to create his new start, but through his hard work and willingness to go through the grieving process, he was able to redefine who he was and what he stood for as a human being.

Sometimes we have to lose ourselves in order to deeply find ourselves. In other words, closure is an inside job. We must learn to let go of what we thought was going to be. We must learn to let go of being totally let down, betrayed, and rejected and come to a place where we can let go of the anger and resentment we initially carried. If we cannot find closure, we cannot overcome our situation, and we will limit our success. There is often no way to closure other than through truly letting go.

Coachable Moment

You can spend minutes, hours, days, weeks, or even months over-analyzing a situation; trying to put the pieces together, justifying what could've, would've happened ... or you can just leave the pieces on the floor and move on.

—*Tupac Shakur*

Persistence

Failure + PERSISTENCE = Overcoming

To succeed we must embrace our inner warrior. We must find the grit to be persistent. We must pull from something deep within ourselves if we are to continue moving forward when facing obstacles. That internal thing we pull from is optimism.

Optimism is magical. It reminds us of our dream, why we are doing what we are doing, and the reasons we started. Optimism funds our persistence. It is the idea of that elusive pot of gold at the end of our story that makes the suffering and hard work we experience along the way so worth it.

The development of persistence doesn't grow solely from our individual journey through suffering done in isolation. Although that is one important way we develop our ability to persist, we are more adept at holding onto our will to persist when we have supportive relationships backing us up. Persistence requires individual will *and* community—even if it's a community of just two. Best-case scenario? To be embraced in a community of people who show diversity in experience, age, outlook, talents, skills, and viewpoints from our own. These differences help cultivate and mature our viewpoints on life. When we have this type of diversity, we receive help and advice in areas where we don't have certain skills but others in our community do. Community offers us a deep sense of emotional and financial safety. It helps us to look beyond ourselves and our own opinions, wants, and needs to grasp the greatness and success that exists beyond our own individual desires. We are able to see we can produce a change that contributes so significantly to others that it makes any and all individual struggles through adversity and challenge worth working through.

To be able to develop a consistency in our persistence, we must appreciate how change and challenge are fundamental to the development of who we are. How we handle change is the marker of our ability to adapt. As we face obstacles, we each have the right and responsibility to examine the roads ahead of us and those we've already traveled. As we take inventory of where we are now, we also have the right to step off any and all negative roads, without feeling any shame or embarrassment, to take another direction. To persist and not burn out, we must cultivate the wisdom to understand that when we cannot change our circumstances, we must change ourselves.

We cannot allow others to say no to us. We must embrace the truth that nothing is insurmountable. There is always more than one way up the same mountain. To persist and be determined is not just about struggling and surviving as much as it is about being resourceful enough to thrive. We must be leaders in our own right and make the choice to dig deep and do what looks unobtainable. Once we see we can do what we thought we couldn't, we naturally become more resilient under stress and pressure. We must embrace the fact that it requires a certain rebelliousness to persist toward what we set out to do regardless of the adversity we face.

To stay on our path, we have to hold old tight to our dreams. Viktor Frankl in his remarkable book *A Man's Search for Meaning* states, "When a man knows the 'why' of his existence he will be able to bear almost any 'how.'" The responsibility we bear in life is always toward others because love, more than success or riches, gives us the deepest and most meaningful reason to keep going. Our 'why' is where persistence resides, and it is what motivates us to stay optimistic. Happiness, persistence, and enthusiasm are greatly increased when we have something to look forward to, so it is imperative to stay focused on our bigger picture when facing obstacles.

Persistence is a virtue to practice and nurture, just like any other. The best way to do this is to nurture our own mind. All great successful people read. When we're in the middle of our more trying times, it is essential we find stories of those who have survived similar trespasses to ours, to find hope, new perspectives, and new ways to go through our own trials. We must make use of great poetry, meaningful stories, music, and movies. All of these resources inspire us back to our purpose. Reading develops our minds and matures our wisdom. Through it we grow in our education and the fortitude we need to stretch in the ways our journey requires. When we cultivate our minds, we foster the depth of our spirit.

To succeed in the ways and levels we desire, we have to stay in motion. To stay in motion, we must gather our bones: We need a backbone, a wishbone, and a funny bone. Our will to persist isn't limited to surviving the depths, terrors, and monotony of the grind. It is also about keeping a hopeful heart, believing in the magic of this Universe, and never losing our sense of humor. If we take ourselves too seriously, we will burn out. We must strive to be as lighthearted as possible. What we dream of should not just comprise suffering and hard work but also intense feelings of joy, anticipation, and excitement. Pressure is a given, but we must not allow pressure to kill our longing. The trick to coping with pressure is not to procrastinate and paralyze our advancement. Advancing is inspired through longing, through joy, and through the ability to stay strong in our convictions.

We have to love ourselves in order to love the journey we're on. It takes a certain seditiousness to speak up for ourselves. Part of being successful means we must speak from our hearts and against unfairness and negativity. The more we persist in championing who we are and the more genuinely we express ourselves, the more we develop that voice from within that can compete with the false and negative judgments cast upon us by other people. When we love ourselves, we laugh more, we smile, and we're more persistent. Wherever there is love or joy, things seem to make more sense and success becomes a bit more effortless. Why? Because when we love what we do and who we are, working is easy. The truer we are to ourselves, the more we draw new opportunities and people into our lives. When we love ourselves and what we do, we have that natural quality of uplifting the morale around us. It is crucial that we love and acknowledge others, to give them hope, and to breathe goodness into them. Anyone who feels deeply valued is much more likely to take ownership of their responsibilities.

It is essential to your persistence that you value yourself. It's the most important thing you can do if you want to succeed in any area of your life. Everything successful and healthy *outside* of you develops directly from what is healthy and successful *inside* of you. The more you love yourself, the more support you have from your community, the more durable you are when things get rough.

You have been endowed with the miraculous. You are one of the true wonders of this world.

And yet, things aren't always going to go your way. So what? Persist anyway.

You cannot allow yourself to underestimate who you are and the good you have to do for others.

Appreciate all people.

Most importantly, never take no for an answer. If you do this, you essentially allow someone else to determine your destiny.

You, and how deeply you love and believe in yourself, are the only real determiners of your excellence.

What Dogged Determination Requires

Commitment in the chase

Persistence and determination lead straight to success. And they require *commitment*. Whatever we pursue must be met with our full attention and nothing less. Hard work must not be something we allow ourselves to shy away from when it could mean losing an opportunity to improve ourselves and our lives. It is this level of commitment that bucks any temptation we may entertain to slack off.

At the same time, I've found that there's value in underestimating what we can achieve and to question if we have what it takes. It's here that begins the romantic *chase* to achieve what seems impossible to us. Who doesn't want to win against all odds? Succeeding isn't always about feeling confident or qualified. It's more emotional than that. Succeeding is about desire. It's about the chase. And what makes the pursuit so intoxicating is wondering all the while if we can really obtain the prize. Success is elusive, and this is part of its attraction and thrill.

To stay determined in the chase, we must view our *past experiences as our most valuable teachers*. Once we have extracted what we were supposed to learn from any given mistake, we leave with a deeper wisdom about why we did what we did and the reasons it did not work. With each mistake, we become more experienced. Our increased experience frees us from having to carry any embarrassment or shame associated with the mistakes we've made. If we ignore our wrongdoings and turn to blame, we get in the way of our own professional expansion and development. As long as we blame, we will continue to repeat the same mistakes. Instead, we should view our mistakes as perfect opportunities to learn something valuable that we didn't understand before, to use these experiences to increase our knowledge.

Coachable Moment
The past doesn't define you, it trains you.
—Unknown

A sense of duty

We must live, work, breathe, and operate in our lives with a sense of duty. Luck has little to do with success or failure. "Luck" is something we create individually. Duty, on the other hand, has to do with our sense of purpose, with giving back, with contributing to others and working hard to do so. We create our own luck through our sense of duty, through persistence, determination, having a positive mental attitude, acting in this world with kindness, and consistently networking for new opportunities. We cannot think much about luck. We must know that if we succeed, it is because we caused it, and if we fail, it is because we caused it. We must take responsibility either way. This approach is much more useful for our personal growth and development than it is to wonder about if or when luck will eventually strike. We must have the faith that with enough time combined with our hard work that things will eventually fall into place. "Luck" is the gift we give ourselves from never giving up.

Prioritizing and organizing

As we wait for our hard work to pay off and for things to start falling into place, we can focus on prioritizing well and staying organized. Determination, like any other virtue, does not come in an unlimited supply. Not every detail of our lives is always going to be under our influence. We must be wise in determining which elements are and are not under our direct control in any given moment so we can focus on prioritizing, pushing, nurturing, promoting, fixing, improving, and maximizing on those elements we can continue to work on.

To achieve this, I suggest that, on any given day, you focus on your urgent 20 percent. When you focus on what is urgent, you get through your bigger stressors more quickly and efficiently, which allows you more freedom to work on the remaining 80 percent—those less important details that serve to distract you and hold you back. Train yourself to work smarter, not just harder, by knowing the difference between what is under your power and what needs to be dismissed as useless worry, concern, or simple distraction. It is easy to focus on the things that do not stress you out and to avoid the things that do. Remove the stress first and you will get more done with more joy and determination.

Support for others

Another important element of staying determined lies in our ability to be happy for and supportive of our network of people. We must be happy for the successes of others and not allow ourselves to see them as takers of our treasure. We must hold the belief that there is enough success, love, beauty, and happiness to go around. When we hold this belief, we eliminate feelings of being diminished as we witness others succeeding. The more they succeed, the more the entire network succeeds—and that includes us. We must advocate for the whole and do all we can to contribute our own individual success to the mix.

Any time you wish for another person to fail, you attract failure to yourself. If we live our lives jealous and spiteful toward others and what they have or don't have, they will sense this in our vibe, through how we talk about ourselves and others, and how we respond when things don't go our way while going great for someone else. A powerful way to prosper for our own success is to be a great supporter of others and their accomplishments. When we are open, willing, and supportive of others, they are more likely to treat us with the same generosity, openness, and support. If we are selfish, others will be less willing to offer us opportunities. For that reason, the resilient among us support the success of others wholeheartedly. In fact, it is important that we spend time around those who are as successful, if not more successful, than we are. As a competitive athlete, I always chose to train with those who were better than I was because it increased my drive to better myself.

I encourage you to Love Up, Live Up, Succeed Up, and Think Up so you can push your growth in a consistent and upward direction. We must first be inspired to succeed from within, and then make it a part of our life's purpose to love and inspire others. The more you support others to succeed, the more you draw increased success and happiness to yourself.

Competition with yourself

Determination doesn't always come through competition with others. There is really no need to be competitive with anyone other than ourselves. If we continue with the idea that we are each unique, then competing with others—what they have, their job titles, salaries, or accomplishments—becomes useless. We can admire and want those things for ourselves, but we have to be competitive with our own goals rather than with other people. In this way, each goal achieved is a competition won. To only focus on competing with others breeds low-level emotions such as envy and resentment. We cannot be successful if we're wasting our time in the trap of comparison because all it does is weaken our spirits and our state of mind.

We must be inspired from within, by measuring ourselves against our own inner desires, goals, and timelines. This approach makes us visionary. It keeps us building ourselves and our visions. The more visionary we become in our goals and dreams, the less we succumb to settling for less in all the important areas of our lives. We must take our short-term goals and make it a point to revisit them as a way to measure our progress. The process of reviewing our goals and desires reminds us of why we are doing what we are doing, and why we're working so hard to do it. To stay determined, we need these reminders.

Positive speech

Our ability to persist and stay determined speaks highly to our composure, confidence, and dignity. We must develop and speak a positive language about our success. Carving out time for "poor me," complaining, whining, and martyring about how things are so bad in our lives will achieve nothing but more negativity. Words have power. The language we speak is the life experience we create. That is how powerful our words are, and how much they can impact our success. We cannot complain our way into succeeding. Complaining has never proven to make people feel better or to help them become more successful, grateful, fulfilled, or happy.

Gratitude

Gratitude is also fundamental to our persistence and determination. When we review our goals and see how far we have come, we must take a moment to be thankful for our growth and progress. Gratitude brings us back to the answers we want to live. As we strive for success, we should expect to feel exhausted. But we can also learn how to transmute our exhaustion into gratitude. Gratitude gives us the meaning we feel we are losing, which returns us to the determined attitude we need to keep moving forward.

Be grateful you have a life you love, goals and visions that spring from your core, and for the love and abundance present in your life.

Be thankful you have a purpose, that you make a difference, that you want to make a difference, and that you're capable of giving, loving, sharing, and advocating for yourself and others.

Be thankful for all the opportunities you have yet to experience.

Be thankful for your failures, as they are your wisdom teachers.

Be thankful you have a life to live and time to use wisely.

Be thankful for it all, and you will become all that you seek to be.

Overcoming

Failure + Endurance = OVERCOMING

We can all overcome.

If we look back on our lives, we can see that we're still here, that we have overcome, and that we're likely better people as a result. Our personal growth and development are superpowers developed from adversity. If we fail, our overcoming is about failing forward. Life's challenges and hardships are the chisels that unleash the true masterpiece each of us embody within. Adversity inspires us to transcend what hurts, what is scary, unfair, or otherwise uncertain. We cannot be defeated if we're determined to continue getting up and to keep moving. Defeat only comes if we quit. When we refuse to view quitting as an option, we possess *transcend-ability*, which is persistence on steroids.

Overcoming is much deeper than bouncing back. In my mind, there is no such thing as "bouncing back" anyway. After all, we cannot return or go back to who we were before the hardship. We've already changed. So we have to fail forward from wherever we've landed.

In a profound way, adversity is a beautiful thing. It sheds light on what is missing in our lives and illuminates the areas in each of us that need improvement.

Without adversity we would never gain the superpower of overcoming. Our hardships are our hope-ships. They sail us from one place to another with each hardship teaching us more of what we need to know to be better and do better. Each hardship brings new information, which means new hope and new direction.

We must train ourselves to discover the blessings in our bummers, to find ways out of our suffering by learning from our suffering. As we become clear on what is missing and what hasn't worked, we discover the keys to what will work going forward.

As we begin to trust the directions our lives take us, we live our dreams more fully.

As we overcome, we become more authentic, more confident, vulnerable, and real. This is what success is all about. The greatest by-product of overcoming is not the end result but how deeply we get to know ourselves.

We are magical, resilient, magnificent human beings. The more we overcome, the more tools we have in our toolkit for execution. The more we persist, the longer we stay around and never give up and the more acknowledgement and recognition we begin to receive. We become known for the strength of our character to find a way when by all accounts there seems to be none.

Through overcoming we come to trust that if we have the will, we will find the way.

MARINATE ON THIS

I saw the angel in the marble and carved until I set him free.

—*Michelangelo*

Part 4
ESTEEM NEEDS

The fact is that people are good, give people affection and security, and they will give affection and be secure in their feelings and their behavior.
—Abraham Maslow

In concert with the need to love and belong is the desire to be recognized for our personal accomplishments. Maslow divides this portion of his theory into external and internal motivators. External motivators are prizes and awards bestowed for our times of outstanding performance, elevation in status (such as a coveted promotion), and newfound attention and admiration from others. Internal motivators are the private goals we set for ourselves (such as beating a prior month's numbers) and the satisfaction of earning self-respect for having done the right thing. We each crave recognition because it brings a fairness to the consistency of our hard work and effort. When we experience that others value what we do, the effort we put in is viewed more logically in that it makes sense we would be acknowledged based on what we have contributed. When we see that our efforts are noticed, we take more pride in our work. The more validated we feel for our efforts, the more inspired we are to set our performance bar even higher. To accumulate feelings of positive esteem, we achieve much, respect ourselves and others, and garner the respect and trust of those who surround us. This grows us into being the person we need to be to sustain our success and live our dreams.

Honesty + Competence = Good Reputation

If I take care of my character, my reputation will take care of me.
—Dwight L. Moody

The kind of character we need for developing a sound reputation cannot be developed in ease and quiet. Good character comes through trial and error, through failure and execution. It is through this unpredictable process that our souls are strengthened, visions cleared, ambitions inspired, and success achieved. Each of us develops a reputation that reflects who we really are, but this takes work (effort), a lot of hard work (persistence), and time (perseverance).

The type of character we build is our choice. If we make poor choices—such as being dishonest, lazy, entitled, egotistical, or bullish—we cannot create a positive reputation. In every situation, we have a choice in how we will respond. Good character is what separates the activator from the procrastinator, the dreamer from the doer, and the successful from the non-successful. When it comes to character, we are not what we think or say; we are what we *do*.

How we behave in our lives is the result of the values we uphold and practice from our heart. Whatever we meditate on in our heart becomes the wellspring of all of our action. We must have a good heart to build a good reputation. If we lie, steal, seek constant attention, or act immorally, it is because we have fostered and nurtured such things from within.

The great news is that because character is a choice, we can choose to change it. If we don't like who we are, we must reinvent ourselves.

Honesty

HONESTY + Competence = Good Reputation

Honesty functions as the soul of our success. We cannot achieve lasting success without it.

Honesty is also the marker of a strong and courageous person. The person who views honesty as a weakness or as something to be taken advantage of will soon learn that honesty can only come from a person brave enough not to cut corners, not to use other people, and not to live off of the rush of short-lived successes.

Without honesty, confidence ultimately ceases to exist. Many people and organizations fail to recognize this truth and end up paying sorely for their short-minded crookedness in a number of ways. Whether it is paid for in humiliation, loss of a steady flow of finances, the total loss of reputation, or the accumulation of unhappy customers, they will pay. Truth is like cream in coffee—it eventually rises to the surface.

Coaching Moment

We learned about honesty and integrity—that the truth matters ... that you don't take shortcuts or play by your own set of rules ... and success doesn't count unless you earn it fair and square.

—*Michelle Obama*

Advantages of Honesty

No matter the environment, when we live honestly, it creates a pervasive and positive ripple effect throughout our lives. People are naturally drawn to honesty because they know they can get the truth delivered to them in a way that also advocates for them. Likewise, when we value honesty, it will affect everyone our lives touch. In business, when honesty is the working foundation, our colleagues will trust us and one another, employees will view our management with less suspicion, and customers will return and spread the word about our integrity.

We have less mess when we choose to act with honesty. We don't have to worry about getting into trouble with the IRS or the media because of unethical behavior. We live clean lives. We operate from respect and the highest levels of integrity.

Wherever there is honesty, there can be no greed, but there is humility.

Coachable Moment

No legacy is so rich as honesty.
—*William Shakespeare*

When Honesty Is Absent

If there is dishonesty at the top of any organization, whether that be in our families or in our work environments, the trickle effect is that it fosters dishonest communication between family members, colleagues, management, and our customers, negatively impacting the way we and others perform. Because of this, every area of our lives and businesses suffer.

Dishonesty is reinforcing because we can get away with it in the short-term, but it is deadly in the long-term. The truth will eventually seep out and expose itself.

Our lives cannot function well under the guise of mistrust. A lack of trust creates anarchy, killing our resilience and the openness of others. Everything becomes competitive rather than collaborative within a group of people that should be coming together around a single goal or purpose. When we think about succeeding, we want to feel hopeful that it will be an honest, collaborative, bonding, and fulfilling process. We must look at leadership as similar to parenting. We must commit to creating a *do-as-I-do* environment, not a *do-as-I-say* one.

The quickest solution to any cover-up is a lie. We lie to try and avoid exposing our mistakes or other trespasses that may be criticized by others. But lies come with an inherent risk—the risk of exposure. You can be sure the truth will surface, and when it does, it will generate disrespect toward those who have been dishonest.

To create an honest environment, you must be committed to truth and reality. When honesty is not valued at the top of any organization, it won't be valued at the bottom. If you want to assess if a person or an organization prizes integrity, look no further than its leadership.

Challenges to Honesty

In today's corporate world where competition is overvalued, it can be difficult to maintain an atmosphere that fosters integrity. Where competition is so highly prized, an atmosphere is created where individual sales or promotions are focused on at the expense of honest behavior. Getting or exceeding our numbers takes precedence over everything else. This makes it easy for deceitfulness to flourish. To counter this and to promote honesty within the workplace, we as the leaders of our own lives must model the behavior we want to see in others.

One of the basic core values of honesty is courage. It is better to lose a short-term deal to make room for a longer-term gain. We must develop the nerve to face the truth and do the right thing simply because it is the right thing to do. This is the marker of our integrity. We have to understand that we are solely responsible for our success and failure, and we cannot expect other people to build our business for us, nor can we lie and take the easy way up the ladder. If we do, we are sure to have someone else take over and take us under.

Let's face it. Dishonesty is unsettling and destructive. You can feel this in your cells when you're being dishonest, and you can often tell when someone is being dishonest with you. It isn't productive to work or live in an environment that is based in a lack of integrity and stepping over others to get to the top. And what exactly is the top of such an organization? The top of a house of paper cards. Solid foundations are not built on lies.

To live a fulfilling and successful life, you must embrace the idea that you are your own brand. So be an honest brand. Be clear and persistent in who you are, where you are headed, and how you handle all your business and personal dealings. When you're honest, you can create and run a flourishing business. Honesty allows people to know where they stand with you, which eliminates guessing, fear, confusion, and wasted time. Use each challenge you face in life, love, or business as a test of your character. Don't use dishonesty as a way to cover-up. Use failure for refinement. This refinement keeps your life, your relationships, and your business clean of negativity. Being upfront keeps you forever pointed in the direction of your dreams. The truth keeps you connected to all that is important and vital.

People gravitate toward what is real. This is why being honest ranks us among the exceptional. When we are honest, we have the internal freedom to live from a simple, upfront, gentle space where we are not afraid of what may sneak up and expose us. Honesty allows us to experience who we really are. And it creates trust in others. They come to see that they can fully depend on us because it is clear that we have no ulterior motives.

To live a life we love, we must wholeheartedly believe that the truth is the only path that will lead us to our success and into genuine, heart-felt intimacy. We must be addicted to our own self-improvement as a way to guarantee we will do things right.

Apologize Whenever Necessary

When we operate with honesty, we understand we are largely a product of the mistakes we've made and the invaluable information we have learned from them. Since all of us are going to make mistakes, we will all have things to apologize for. It takes uprightness to offer a genuine apology. Whether we have used our words or actions harmfully, or we have omitted information that exposed itself and really hurt someone, we owe it to ourselves and others to apologize. When we can acknowledge our mistakes and can say any combination of three different three-word statements—"I am sorry," "I was wrong," or "You were right"—we start to heal what was broken. From a place of sorrow and empathy, we are able to make the changes necessary to do better and be better going forward. Genuine remorse helps rebuild trust between ourselves and those we've hurt. If this type of moral behavior is infused in upper management, it is this type of behavior that will permeate every tier of the business below. Any time there is an apology, there is transparency and an opportunity for a fresh start.

Coachable Moment

There is a big difference between a real apology and a fauxpology, one is genuine and one is dishonest. As a psychologist, I unfortunately see the fauxpology much more often than I see the genuine apology. Let me offer you the anatomy of what a genuine apology looks like: "I did X, and I should not have done it. I apologize without defense. I will do Y to make amends and/or make sure what I did doesn't happen again." Now, of course there may be reasons given for why things went down as they did, but you will be able to trust they were more careless in their actions than vicious. If a person apologizes like this, it is authentic. When a person can never be wrong, the word "sorry" may be used, but the "sorry" will land as a criticism of you, either direct or implied.

—*Danu Morrigan*

Fresh starts, healing, bonding, reconnecting, and trust cannot develop when honesty is absent.

Honesty and humility make us extraordinary people. These are the magical qualities we want backing every area of our lives where we seek to feel successful, fulfilled, and satisfied. Success that sustains over time is always, without exception, built upon trusted and dependable relationships. When we can mend what has been misunderstood or broken, we collectively carry on even stronger than before.

Ask for Advice

If we want to live from honesty, we must view ourselves as life-long learners. We must never assume we know it all. Essential to honesty is to possess the humility to seek advice whenever necessary. If we don't know what to do in a situation, the advice of others helps direct our thoughts and actions. When we ask to be shown what to do, we implicitly show the other person that we trust their experience, skills, knowledge, insight, expertise, and opinions. There are times in life we will need more support and advice from others than we typically would. In certain situations we may even require to be taught, trained, or even further educated to accomplish what we've set out to do. When we ask for advice, we automatically create a collaborative relationship. When we're honest, we're also naturally more modest. We understand that needing advice is temporary, but the knowledge we gain from learning is forever.

Asking for help should never be below you. No one is superior to anyone else in God's eyes. When you ask for help, you reveal your humanity. You show you are vulnerable and that you have no need to pretend you have all the information. This subtle act makes others more comfortable in their own vulnerabilities. When you ask for help, you get it, and in the process, you demonstrate your humility, respect, and willingness to listen to others. All of these qualities are markers of excellence.

For a business to thrive, it has to be a motivating and pleasant place to be. We want to surround ourselves with others who must want those around us to have the desire to wake up and do their part. An open and honest environment drives this motivation.

There are no short cuts when it comes to life, love, or success, so don't take any. Any negotiation or communication performed under the guise of dishonesty will wreak havoc later down the road. You will likely be confronted when the people you promised things to feel disappointed, confused, angry, or let down.

So create an honest environment.

Let go of short-term benefits to land the bigger and longer-term goals or relationships worth waiting for. It's the metaphor of the tortoise and the hare. The hare starts fast, burns bright, wears out, and fizzles fast. The turtle, however, takes a steady, slower pace, and is more resilient and consistent. And it's the turtle that ends up winning the race.

Seek to win. Work with the longer view in mind. And do it all with honesty. Then integrity will reign.

Competence
Honesty + COMPETENCE= Good Reputation

Our competence is the purest reflection and expression of our abilities, commitments, knowledge, and skill, which enable us to perform effectively in most situations. It shows we have sufficient knowledge and abilities and that we have taken responsibility for our expertise. The more competent we are, the deeper our insight into how to most effectively respond to the various situations we face.

Competence is not about being better than others. It is about being the best at what *we* do. To achieve success on any level, we must become experts in our own field. With our knowledge and expertise, there should be very few questions we cannot answer or problems we cannot investigate and solve. And the more competent we are, the more confident we become.

Intrapreneurial Potential

What does *intrapreneurial* mean? To be intrapreneurial means that we cultivate our individuality under the umbrella of corporate America. We need to be willing to go inside ourselves and generate ideas that may break the status quo. It is too easy to become robotic and follow the external rules and ideas set out in front of us in the corporate world. To be intrapreneurial, we access the reservoirs of our internal wisdom, instincts, and openness to visualize unforeseen opportunities that exist within our field before others are even aware they are needed. This is the gift of being knowledgeable. Because we can count on our base knowledge, it frees up our mind to think more creatively about how to maximize upon ideas that already exist or generate new ones we can build on.

Train yourself to become aware that ideas can come from anywhere and are available at all times. By becoming alert to this fact and learning how to seize upon the ideas you discover or generate, you will gain the ability to live outside of the status quo and become a pioneer in your field. You will become known as a boundary pusher and a leader others will want to follow and listen to.

When you feel competent, you are self-driven and more unafraid to risk failure because you have created a solid base to "fail" into. And as your risks are rewarded, your success will continue to rise and expand. This will allow you to operate even more out of your creative genius, which will turn you into a person your organization and others in your field will grown to depend on. When we're good at what we do, we become a strategic influencer of others. We are able to persuade, inspire, and gather support because we have earned a reputation people trust.

A solid sense of competence allows for more risk because we possess the necessary confidence in our skills and in our knowledge to live with a balanced optimism. We are able to rise above the negativity, yet we are not Pollyannas; we are wise to the concept of risk and reward. Because of this, we're able to overcome our temporary moods and emotional states well enough to press through them, making us more dependable and steady. We are able to receive criticism while continuing to move on without allowing our ego to destroy us through unnecessary or unprofessional emotional reactions. With a strong sense of competence, our passion and knowledge become enough to move us forward and to overcome roadblocks.

Competency in Business

For our lives and businesses to thrive, our own well-roundedness, knowledge, skills, education, and training must be our first and ongoing priority. To be competent, our desire to learn and grow must never have an expiration date. We must continually develop ourselves to become increasingly better problem-solvers where we are able to predict challenges we may face. Problem-solving requires critical, innovative, and often creative thinking strategies that allow us to navigate through crises and solve them. We must use our skill and knowledge to help us remain calm and act quickly. All of this will be critical to our success. Business is always going to be fluid and changing by nature, making it in need of consistent refinement and upkeep to generate improvement. This is the most fulfilling part of any journey and should not be viewed as a drag. If we allow ourselves and our business to be in a consistent state of improvement, our business remains adaptable and competitive. We can achieve this with little to no expense other than a little extra time and attention. We must infuse this perspective and approach to our work into those who work for us. For as each person improves, the company improves, bringing greater satisfaction to all concerned.

Coachable Moment

Success on all levels is the most heartfelt when it is earned by one's own ability to shift, change, and improve.

—Dr. Sherrie Campbell

Invest in Self-Examination

Success takes a team of people. We cannot carry the burden of success alone. We need others.

We need them for support, education, training, and advice.

We need them for their energy, their sense of humor, and their skills and talents.

We need them to fall back on when we run out of steam.

We need others to help put us back on our feet, headed in the right direction. None of us are above these needs.

And when we have people advocating for us, it directly increases our self-confidence and our ability to perform at the peak performance levels necessary to increase our own competency, happiness, and success.

What follows are eight ways we benefit from gathering a team of support around us.

1) Acknowledgement

We all need others to acknowledge our dignity, worth, and value.

So often people treat us as things, as mere objects. They label us as this or that and neglect to treat us as human beings. We cannot connect with a person who treats us as an it or a thing, as something to use or get around. It's demoralizing and depersonalizing to be minimized this way.

But when we have a coach or a therapist or someone else advocating for us, teaching us, supporting us, and even confronting us, we feel as if we are being encountered as a whole human being—as a person of worth, intelligence, and significance. When we are acknowledged for our dignity, we feel *seen*.

We all deserve to be acknowledged for who we are and for what we do, and to be told why who we are and what we do matters.

2) Touch

Appropriate physical and light touch (for example, a handshake, hug, touch on the shoulder, high-five, fist pound, or kiss on the cheek), direct eye contact, and attentiveness do more to connect two people than virtually anything else. When we are touched in such ways, we are recognized as worthy, likable, and valuable.

It is good for us to be pulled away from our electronic devices to experience a brick-and-mortar, in-person encounter with another human being—to see their face, to look into their eyes, and to have an emotional exchange. Such human touches stimulate our mood hormones responsible for trust and bonding. These appropriate forms of touching make us feel special. And when we feel special, we feel more competent in life as a whole.

3) Advice

When other people advocate for us, they see our competencies and lead us toward them. They look beyond themselves and focus on us.

A good coach or therapist can only advise us well if they are able to listen to us and observe us objectively. When this attunement is present, they can help us determine what directions are in our best interest. The more we are guided to lead from our strengths, the more competent we become.

Advocating has nothing to do with being criticized, judged, or invalidated, all of which are negative and nonproductive. We cannot be cut down, pressured, or demoralized into developing competency.

We need coaches and therapists focused on guiding us, brainstorming with us, and exploring all of our possibilities. When we are advised in this way, we are guided according to our own desires rather than according to someone else's agenda. Advice coming from a selfish agenda is poor advice because it is not serving us or our needs. Instead, it is more about our coach or therapist using us in some form to meet their own ideas of success. When we are with the right people, we are advised to reach for and achieve the goals that we have established for ourselves.

4) Support

Support generally comes in the simplest ways. We each crave time, love, and attention. When we go to someone for support, we do not need them to fix or solve our problems. Rather, we go to them so they can hold the space for us to vent, be in fear, and express our more reactive and worried emotions around the problem. Once we have expelled these emotions, we have the space to be more innovative and to engage in the brainstorming process. When we are in that space, our coach or therapist holds the belief that things will turn out okay for us, even when we cannot hold that belief for ourselves. They act as our net. A great coach or therapist encourages us into our own self-reflection by asking us questions that lead us to our own answers. It is through our *own* answers that we build our expertise. When we receive this support, we come to experience, without humiliation, that we can be in our own negative drama in front of another person who will support us to find ourselves and our way to a more productive process.

5) Coaches and therapists

We are the most successful when we are coached to achieve our dreams.

Believe it or not, those who support us to achieve our dreams are also in the process of living their own since their helping us is a part of their own dream. As we succeed and become more competent, at the hands of their guidance, so they succeed and become more competent. Goals are a shared experience.

When we have someone in our corner, we develop the tough-mindedness and confidence to go out in the world and do our best.

When we experience missteps, we have someone in our corner to support and coach us with improved strategies that build our competencies and then push us back out there to succeed and conquer.

As for myself, I see both a shrink and a coach for two reasons. My coach and I have an attack approach, and my therapist helps me download the deeper parts of my psyche that either help or hinder my progress. Both individuals help me lead from my strengths rather than encouraging me to overcompensate for my perceived weaknesses. They serve totally different purposes, but what each of them contributes makes a tremendous difference in my life.

Yes, I am a shrink who sees a shrink. How can I lead people into their own growth or out of their suffering if I am not actively pursuing my own development?

One of the first questions I would ask a therapist, when shopping for one, is if he or she is in therapy as well. After all, how valuable is it to follow a leader who has never suffered?

Humble yourself. We all need people to cheer us on, to advocate for us, to make us think, recommend us to others, and acknowledge us publicly. We all need people in our corner advocating for our growth and success.

Coachable Moment

Every great athlete has a coach. Power lifters are able to lift heavier weights when they have a spotter. Every person driven towards success would do best to have a coach, a therapist, a mentor, or all of the above to guide and support them in living out their goals personally and professionally.

—*Dr. Dave White*

6) Believe

When we trust someone's belief in us, it makes us even more driven to live up to what that person sees in an effort to prove him or her correct. Our success is better sustained when we have someone advocating for us. We become more resilient the more we are encouraged, supported, and believed in because we are succeeding and exploring from a foundation of love, not fear. Having strong support behind us lifts our spirits. When our spirits are high, we undoubtedly handle stress and conflict better.

7) Expectation

People naturally live up or down to expectations. When we are held to high, reachable expectations, we will reach as far and as wide as we must to live up to what is expected. High expectations covertly communicate that we have the ability to do whatever we desire. The expectations from those who are on our team will naturally push us out of our comfort zone, causing us to become curious about what we are really capable of achieving. Our curiosity, backed by another's support and belief, influences us so deeply that we naturally begin to test the edges of our fears and rise up into new and broader levels of competency.

8) Reframe

All of us suffer from differing amounts of negative self-talk, which is one reason our coaches and therapists help us learn to speak a new language—the language of *possibility*. They remind us of and keep us in touch with the magic of our own inner power and ability.

The most important way someone can advocate for us is to focus our minds on solutions to our problems rather than on all the problems within a problem. Moving forward from a problem-focused mind-set only creates more problems. But when our negative self-talk is reframed, we learn healthier and more empowering ways to be in relationship with ourselves, our circumstances, and others. We come to understand that every no takes us one step closer to the yes we are looking for. We are shown solid, justifiable reasons for staying in the grind when frustrations seem to be taking us over. The more we grind, the more competent we become. We must have someone teaching us to never accept no for an answer, and we must be encouraged to say yes to new ideas, new behaviors, new information, and new skills that have the potential to stretch and grow us in all the right ways.

The more competent we are, the easier life becomes. When we are experts at what we do, and we feel certain about who we are and what we can do, we are knowledgeable enough to provide the required information. And if for some reason we don't have immediate answers, we will know where to turn to find them.

To live a successful life and own a thriving business, we must be knowledgeable in running a business that works. We must be intrapreneurial. We must possess a depth of understanding in knowing how our organization works so we have room to be creative in expanding our outreach with new ideas and visions. We become visionary in ways that maximize the already existing potential of our company or product.

At the very core, we must love what we do. Just like anything else, passion needs upkeep, and that is why we hire a team of mentors and advisers who help keep us inspired and moving forward. The best of the best use *applied knowledge.*

Good Reputation
Honesty + Competence= GOOD REPUTATION

Our reputation is an "animal" that is largely designed by a committee of thought from those outside of us. We give birth to it, but the way in which it actually develops is dependent on the actions and perceptions of others. Our reputation is nearly a totally separate entity from who we are. It represents the collective idea or the projection everyone else shares about us. Our reputation is based partially on our own actions but mostly upon the perceptions other people have of our actions. Therefore, we can influence our reputation but we cannot control it. This is exactly what makes the building of our reputation so exposed to vulnerability and collapse.

Our reputation can help us or hurt us. And when it helps us, it can be incredibly beneficial. While we cannot stop others from being jealous of us or slandering us, our reputation comes to our rescue when our supportive networks rise to our defense, even when we are unaware that this is happening on our behalf.

We are all caretakers of one another's reputations. In a society in which simply being accused is enough to render a conviction in the court of public opinion, we would all do well to presume not only innocence but goodness until facts prove otherwise. It benefits all of us to be kinder and gentler with one another. When we are this way with one another, we become more likable, and this helps make our social support networks stronger and our reputations more solid.

To build a great reputation, we have to be a person who deserves one. We must commit to taking consistent action that embodies the image we want others to associate us with.

The image we want cannot be false or made-up and used like a billboard advertisement. For a reputation to be sustained, the image we build must be authentic to who we are as a person; it must reflect the truth and depth of our character, which means we must be honest and competent in the areas that we say we are.

It is best not to be boastful in promoting ourselves. We must work hard enough to guarantee that our success and character speak for themselves. When we succeed quietly, people become curious and seek to know who we are, what we do, and how we did what we did. They desire to discover our true character. In this way, our own good reputation provides us a consistent target at which to keep aiming.

Sometimes we may not feel we deserve our reputation, that it's better than we are. But we must allow this to inspire and motivate us to continue to improve ourselves. Our good reputation will inspire others as well. There is nothing more beautiful or powerful than that—to have an impact on others that is so moving that it leads them to discover themselves and their own potential. We all need positive role models, even the best and brightest among us. And if we can become one of those role models for others, that's all the better.

A reputation is a fragile thing because honesty and competency naturally wax and wane. Let's face it: we are not perfectly competent each day, each week, or each month. Nor are we perfectly honest each day or in each situation when we may be feeling fear or shame for one reason or another. We are human, which makes our reputation a fragile thing. Consequently, our reputation requires our constant nurturing. Consistency is crucial. We must aspire to live up to our reputation. We especially cannot risk damage to our reputation if the person we let down is highly influential in our network. Of course, failure is a part of life, including successful lives. We will sometimes let people down. But that in and of itself is not enough to damage our reputation if we handle our failure in ways that truly reflect our integrity, humility, persistence, and other good qualities we have formed. When we strive to be the person we most want to be, a good reputation will naturally come out of that. Even an occasional failure won't upend it.

When we possess the deepest sense of integrity and humbly view ourselves as the underdog, we become the most driven to achieve our dream. When we see ourselves as the underdog, complacency is not a viable option. The chase to be good enough and to develop the reputation we desire will hold tremendous meaning.

A reputation is like a butterfly: beautiful to watch but hard to capture. It must be worked for and perfected like a gorgeous piece of art with attention paid to every detail.

Once our reputation is established, it becomes a more natural desire to want to lead others. We have been led, supported, loved, and coached. Career, now that we are more established, becomes less about us and more about how we can teach, coach, and lead others to develop their own incredible careers, lives, and reputations.

In the leadership role, we are the most vulnerable because we are more visible. We must watch for greed and selfishness and maintain the high integrity of the character that we have built. This will be the driving force to take us and those we lead to newer and more profound heights.

MARINATE ON THIS

It takes 20 years to build a reputation and five minutes to ruin it. If you think about that, you'll do things differently.

— *Warren Buffett*

People + Resilience = Leadership

To handle yourself, use your head. To handle others, use your heart.
—Eleanor Roosevelt

eadership is a reflection of successes achieved, acknowledgments given, one's work ethic, the ability to persist and overcome, and the development of one's reputation. All of these building blocks can grow us into great leaders.

Great leadership, however, doesn't have a single definition. Great leaders have many traits in common. In life or business, leadership is the ability to make good decisions and to encourage others to perform their roles and duties correctly and passionately. Exceptional leaders possess the ability to guide people. They are also dynamic, passionate, and, above all else, great communicators. Great leaders are self-confident, wise, have suffered, and know their way through difficult times. They are charismatic and have an innate ability to influence people. Because of these qualities, they are able to effectively and passionately manage and guide other people.

Leadership is an art. It is constantly changing based on both the people involved and the circumstances at hand. Leadership is a process of consistently adjusting people's behavior to help maximize them to their fullest potential. The greatest leaders we have act as allies to their team members. They work alongside them on the frontlines rather than bearing over them as cold dictators. They are in the grind with their people, shoulder to shoulder, overseeing, guiding, pushing, encouraging, inspiring, and advocating for their team toward success. They do not expect perfection, but they do expect the best of what each team member brings to the playing field. We must never expect that anyone we work with, including ourselves, will just know what they're supposed to be doing. Therefore, to be great leaders, we must take the time needed to ensure our team members are on the same page with us. When we tell our team exactly what we want and expect, they are more driven to go hunt for it and provide it for us. The clearer we are, the more successful our entire network will be.

For us to be great leaders, we must be sure that each person in our network receives opportunities to lead and to shine in his or her own right. Success cannot come from bondage; it can only manifest from freedom and experimentation.

As their leader, we must be emotionally intelligent enough to bend our communication style to click with another person's personality. We must strive to figure out the emotional language each person speaks and learn to communicate in ways that empower them to be at their best.

We must also maintain a protective role with them and love them as we would an extended family of people we've been given the honor to direct.

Most importantly, we must appreciate those we lead. We must appreciate them for who they are and what they contribute. Appreciation goes a long way when it comes to success and happiness. We do not want our team members to just be successful; we must want them to be authentically happy.

The making of a great team comes down to love. We must love what we do, they must love what they do, and when this love is present, we create an environment where everyone has the chance to thrive. This is what true support is all about.

People Skills
PEOPLE SKILLS + Resilience = Leadership

At its core, a happily lived life can be broken down into having a purpose and having significant and loving relationships. To live successfully, we must master the art of charting our own path in tandem to developing relationships that are mutually beneficial and based in integrity, caring, and sharing. We must be good with people and good to people if we are to lead them. When we have a genuine love for people, we become someone others feel compelled to follow and connect with. We must be involved in every aspect of our business, supporting those we work with in any way we can. We must promote the idea of interconnectedness and providing people with a sense of equal value. When people admire us for the essence of who we are and how we built our success, we are in a position to coach and teach them.

A Positive Attitude Increases Success Altitude
Attitude first starts with you.

The most critical step we take toward succeeding at the higher levels is to be mindful of the thoughts that control and dictate the vibe we put out. If we don't like people, people will feel it. It's that simple. If we don't like what we do, people will sense it. Our attitude is everything.

We cannot inspire if we are not inspired.

We cannot lead others if we cannot effectively lead ourselves.

Our attitude communicates our biases and judgments, our openness and pliability, and our perceptions surrounding success and failure. The great thing is that our attitude is our choice and always under our direct construction.

To train our attitude we must call upon our inner coach. This is that voice from within that is able to see for us what we can't yet see for ourselves. It is the voice that boosts us into believing in the unbelievable. When our attitude is nonproductive, we must commit to coaching ourselves through the ruts. We are all capable of reprogramming our fearful, defeatist thinking into thoughts charged with power, conviction, and faith and all directed toward our abilities to meet our goals. The better we coach ourselves, the better and more powerfully we can lead and coach others. The winning formula for our attitude looks like this:

$$EA \text{ (energy of attitude)} \rightarrow Motion \text{ (e-motions)}$$

This formula tells us that the energy of our attitude is carried through our emotions. Because emotions are infectious, we must respect how powerful they are in having an incredibly positive impact or a very negative one. We must use positive self-talk to add positive energy into the views we hold about ourselves, our abilities, our financial gains, our losses, and how we view people and working with them. When the energy we generate comes across as solid and confident, this has a positive impact on everyone around us.

To be the standout exception, we must live to *feel* what it feels like to be extraordinary. We must open our minds to what it means to be different from the rest. As long as we hold a great attitude and avoid believing in limits, we will each experience that *anything* is possible. The only ceiling above us is the one we create ourselves.

To inspire our attitude into the extraordinary, we must use our formula and put our positive emotional energy into motion. One way to accomplish this is to determine what our incentives are at each new step in our goal-setting process. We must ask what results we are moving toward. To determine our incentives, we must think back to what first inspired us to change our life and pursue our goals. What was our incentive then? What is it now? Is it financial gain, self-perseveration, stability, anger, achieving, success, or fear? When our incentives are clear, they shift our attitude to positive. It is easier to put energy toward our goals when we are clear about the desired outcomes we want to achieve. With this type of movement, backed by excitement and clarity, our attitude becomes contagious and infused with our inner power, enthusiasm, and passion. When our attitude is positive, everything is enhanced. Our outlook on business is elevated. We walk faster, smile more, and carry a posture of assuredness, which draws even more success our way. When we hold a positive and infectious attitude, the higher we soar into new levels of success and the happier of a life we live.

Coachable Moment

Virtually nothing is impossible in this world if you just put your mind to it and maintain a positive attitude.

—Lou Holtz

When we're driven and excited about what our purpose is in this world, we are not the people suffering from the Sunday blue's as the new workweek approaches. Instead, we look forward to Monday because we're hungry to get out there and work hard. Our excitement is God-given.

When we work from (or for) our own spiritual enhancement, work is experienced as nurturing to our business and even more so to our soul. The deeper of a connection we feel to our purpose, the more we're willing to suffer for it, and the more we experience the effects of our positive attitude being expressed through us toward everything we do. We can be lighthearted *and* successful. We can work hard from a spirit of lightheartedness in tandem with a soul-driven intensity. Having a lighthearted attitude is invaluable when inspiring others. We must find the humor and lighter side of life as we climb the ladder of success. Whenever we come from love, the heart is light, more open, and more forgiving. Lightheartedness decreases our stress and the stress and pressures of those around us. The less stress an environment holds, the more productively everyone works.

If we are low on energy or our hearts become too heavy, the quick solution to getting our energy back in motion is to engage in physical activity. If we are stressed, physical activity provides a quick release and works to cleanse a negative thought pattern by redirecting it to helping us see the positive. Exercise (or movement of any sort) lifts us into an altered state of mind, increasing our optimism. If we cannot hit the gym on a stressful day, there is no reason we cannot get out of the office and take a fifteen minute walk to shift our mental paradigm. When we change our physiology, we immediately exude an aura of positivity, which has another immediate impact of positively benefiting the work we do and the interactions we have with others. When we master our inner world, we dominate our outer world.

The Power of a Negative Attitude

When driving for success, we cannot get there greedily. Greed will eventually destroy us. If all we think about is our own selfish needs for success, we will start to see people as things rather than as people. Consider the movie *Beauty and the Beast*. The owner of the castle was so self-centered and greedy that when he was cursed and turned into a beast, his castle turned into a dungeon, and the people who lived in that castle were reduced to objects or things to be used.

When others feel disposable, we cannot create a positive working environment or inspire people to jump into our mission. We not only want to be respected for our intelligence and insight but also for our ability to bring out the best in the people around us. Our mission must be shared. It must be inclusive. And it must be done with a loving and positive attitude. So share everything. Share your drive, your thoughts, your feelings, your success, and, most importantly, your heart. When you live with this idea of inclusion, all people will feel important. This is how we need to run our lives and businesses.

We must never ignore or minimize the emotional climate of our work environment. We are the most successful when we create an environment where communication is safe and open. We must allow for frustrations to be vented without mocking, humiliating, ignoring, or minimizing anyone. When we mishandle what others are expressing, we essentially tell them that what they feel, think, and believe are insignificant. Internal chaos and mistreatment lead to missed opportunities. Consistency is essential in our treatment of others. We must verbalize our expectations, so those who work for us or with us know how to respond appropriately. All of us (usually unconsciously) live up or down to expectation, so we must make our expectations clear. When we have defined roles, no one is left confused about what to do.

Putting others down is never going to be a recipe for success. Success is a collective experience. Therefore, we must be generous in giving praise, offering a listening ear, and being supportive of those we are working with or for. This is what we would want others to do for us, right?

Moreover, we should not stay in a career or any other environment where we are being put down. It is of the utmost importance to respect others, which means that we need to be respected too. No one can succeed when feeling oppressed or fearful. We succeed when we feel encouraged, valued, and supported and have a sense of belonging to something.

We must inspire others to want to work together. We must come from a belief in miracles rather than believing that the ideas of other people are ridiculous and far-fetched. The most successful people are those who didn't shrink or dismiss their innovative or "crazy" ideas just because others couldn't see their vision.

At the same time, it's also true that every team needs a certain amount of optimal frustration to be able to grow and develop the resiliency necessary for further success. If as a leader you insert yourself into every move the team makes, the team cannot learn to navigate the sharper edges of conflict, persistence, or the goal-attainment necessary to achieve your desired levels of success. To be a successful entrepreneur, you must know who you are, what your goals are, how to deal effectively with people, and to have the deep understanding that any unbalance in you will be reflected in your team's ability to succeed. Avoid the pitfalls of being over or under controlling. Successful businesses, which stand the test of time, are run by leaders who know when to be firm and when to give some rope. The best way to develop your team is to infuse them with rewards for deserving behavior and letting them fail when necessary so they can learn the skill of getting back up. Be there for them and support them with a sense of trust regardless of the challenges you all will face together along the climb to the top.

Empathy Is the Key

The greatest people on earth—those who leave the most significant impact on others—have empathy. In fact, balanced, healthy, productive relationships can only develop if we can see the world through another person's eyes.

Empathy isn't something we learn in a book. It is developed from our suffering, our willingness to look at the hurt, and our acceptance that anguish is a part of life. We must come to view our times of suffering as essential to the development of empathy. Without empathy, we are extremely limited in working well with anyone, in developing a good reputation, or with becoming a person who can successfully lead others.

For empathy to rule in our lives, consideration must come before accusation. Empathy is life's most authentic healer. It is the emotion that validates people and helps them move out of feeling stuck. When empathy is not present, solutions are forced rather than powerful.

Empathy must be the guiding force behind all of our communication. When we use empathy, it becomes the catalyst for change. Empathy makes communication a two-way, collaborative, reflective process.

Empathy is also truly magical. It allows for vulnerability. It gives people the knowledge that we are capable of putting ourselves in their shoes, thereby truly understanding what they are thinking and feeling. When people feel understood, they experience a huge release. The walls of self-protection they put up immediately fall down.

If empathy is lacking, the walls of self-protection grow higher and thicker. People cannot feel a sense of trust, safety, or security if their points of view aren't seen, validated, implemented, or respected.

Empathy is one of the main principles underlying theories of mindfulness and emotional intelligence, and it is the very fabric of making others feel a sense of satisfaction in a relationship.

Empathy is also the emotion responsible for self-compassion. We are all too hard on ourselves, and oftentimes this transfers out to us being too hard on others. We must be mindful to accept ourselves as human, flaws and all. This makes it easier for us to accept and appreciate others and their flaws.

It's critical to care about how other people are. It's such a simple thing to ask others how they are doing, what they need, and what they feel. When we do this, we connect. When we have a clear idea of how others feel about themselves and what they're doing, it helps us better support and guide them. When we or others feel supported, it is exciting because we realize we are not on our journey alone or without help. We must keep in mind that if we want others to be invested in what we're communicating and to respond cooperatively, we must consider their ideas and their thoughts about who we are and our leadership. When we have this information, we can choose to be defensive or we can learn. It's always a better choice to learn, to grow, and to pivot when necessary. We must use empathy to guide all aspects of our lives, allowing it to influence not only what we say but also how we say what we say and to direct us to the kinds of question we need to ask to pull from the greatness within others. When we take these steps, backed with empathy, it inspires, nurtures, and develops empathy within others.

We must seek to validate the strengths in others. We can easily help a stuck person become unstuck through the simple act of allowing him or her the space to be in the stuck emotions. Empathy removes resistance and breaks down barriers. Helping another can be accomplished by simply validating their experience as a normal response to the adverse situation they are experiencing. In the movie *Inside Out*, the character Sadness is first perceived as a total drag, but by the end of the movie Sadness is the game changer, the healing star of the movie. She is able to give Bing Bong the empathy he needs to move out of his own sadness to help heal the little girl they are trying to save from an emotional breakdown. This movie shows us that we would never know the depths of joy or the wisdom of our hearts if we didn't have the experience of Sadness. In this movie Sadness is the embodiment of empathy, and it demonstrates how powerful empathy is when it comes to healing. As soon as the little girl's parents empathize with her painful experience of moving to a new city, her emotions receive the validation, concern, and attention they needed. She then avoids a horrific breakdown, starts to heal, and begins to embrace her new life in a new home. The lesson we can all learn from this is how important it is to take a moment and give other people some reflection, validation, and understanding. Their protective guards will then drop and healing can begin. The more empathetically we live, the more we model this for others, and the more this becomes the new standard of treatment along our journey to success.

You must understand that empathy is most easily sacrificed when you're upset, angry, or disappointed with another person. You tend to be the most hurtful and impatient in these situations. And because you are human, you will have such moments. The important thing to practice is taking a moment to get clear before speaking. There is nothing wrong with telling someone a conversation needs to wait until you feel clear in your own emotions, in what your position is, and in how and what you need to communicate.

It is also important to take note of the company you keep. If you are dealing with a person incapable of empathy, you must separate from that person. All it takes is one toxic individual to short-circuit your entire path to success. Part of succeeding is knowing who you need to get rid of as much as it is knowing who you need to keep. It is impossible to work with someone who is constantly defensive and unwilling to listen to others. Collaboration, cooperation, teamwork, and success are virtually impossible to achieve when working with these types of people.

Empathy and Success

Empathy must come from our core. It is what makes relationships genuine and complete. Because success is largely built upon a foundation of great relationships, having empathy makes sense.

However, we must not confuse empathy with being a pushover. Being empathetic doesn't mean we sacrifice what we believe to be correct. We can disagree with another person and still be empathetic. We can validate what others say but still maintain the integrity of our own separate view of the situation. Empathy isn't about using everything we validate about another's viewpoint in sacrifice of what we know to be right. It is more about having the strength in our own identity to hear all sides and to analyze the information we're given in a nonbiased, open manner. The goal is to create an empathetic environment for a meeting of the minds to come together to mutually brainstorm and collaborate.

When we face situations that may be more contentious or where we do not come to a meeting of the minds, we must break the interaction down to the golden rule: *Treat people the way we would want to be treated.* We must put ourselves in the thought process of another and ask ourselves how we would like to be treated in their situation and do our best to act that way. We must think about what we're doing and saying if we are to be effective in life, love, or business. The more empathy we bring to our more challenging relationships, business negotiations, or disciplinary situations, the more successful we will be.

Coachable Moment

When you show deep empathy toward others, their defensive energy goes down, and positive energy replaces it. That's when you can get more creative in solving problems.

—*Stephen Covey*

The kindness of your personal spirit—how you treat, think about, and speak to others—makes all the difference when it comes to developing positive and successful relationships. Make sure to lead from your heart and to come from a genuine, open, and sensitive place. If you want to be exceptional, be kind. Let empathy dictate your every word, deed, and action. When you have empathy, you are able to be kind even to those you do not care for. This is not a weakness or a vulnerability. To be empathetic is your superpower. There is truly no human quality that will take you further in life than empathy.

Do not strive just to be successful. Strive to be exceptional. Anyone can be successful. To be exceptional is a more wholehearted experience, where you leave a positive imprint on all of those whose lives you touch.

Be Unselfish

The final topic to address regarding the importance of people skills to leadership is the idea of giving back. *We truly get more out of giving than getting.* When we give back, it increases our own quality of life, our perception of what we have and who we are, and reminds us to be thankful as we begin to see the amazing impact we have on the lives of others. When we give back, we feel good. In giving we are instantly reminded of all the love and abundance we have in our own lives, inspiring us to continue to strive to perform at our peak levels so we have even more to give back. The harder we work, the more we have to give. The more we have to give, the more motivated we become to work harder to give that much more.

The most beautiful thing giving back offers to the giver and the receiver is it builds safe and trusting relationships. It is through an involvement in our communities that we discover and develop mutually satisfying connections and relationships. It's one thing to be lovable, but it's a whole other thing to be Love Able. Love is the most natural emotion. It's the emotion we most enjoy giving and receiving. If we give our love to a person or group of people who will happily take it but not share it in return, we are giving to those who are not Love Able. They do not have the ability to love. Love is not a give-take dynamic but a give-give dynamic. People want to be linked with others who are giving. People want to work for people and companies that care.

We must strive to be remembered, not by how much we earned, but by how much we gave.

Coachable Moment

I've learned that people will forget what you said, people will forget what you did, but people will never forget how you made them feel.

—*Maya Angelou*

Furthermore, when you give of yourself to others in some form or another, it makes those people, whether loved ones or employees, desire to be more productive. When you're loving, it inspires others to be the same way. So be loving.

I truly believe love is the answer to healing of any kind. Empathy, humility, kindness, and understanding all come from love. There is nothing more appealing to others than to be in the presence of a loving person. The truly exceptional know they must love themselves in order to have endless amounts of love to give. Love is a verb. It expresses itself through your loving-kindness, touch, smile, and a sense of your inner joy and vitality. This love is what you must share. If you can do this, success will more naturally and easily manifest in your life and in all the lives your love touches.

We must let there be nothing we wouldn't do to help if we are able. We must take this loving approach into every area of our lives, from our career to our parenting.

≈\\\⁄≈

Coachable Moment

To live a pure unselfish life, one must count
nothing as one's own in the midst of abundance.
—Buddha

≈/\\\≈

Resilience

People Skills + RESILIENCE = Leadership

Resilience is that indefinable quality of strength and fortitude within us that allows the light to break through the cracks. Resilience is more enduring than both skill and talent and is the x-factor that helps us outlast others. Resilience is our ability to return to our own inner stability after a traumatic event. It is the process by which we achieve adaptability. Resilience is what moves us from the feelings of being victimized and powerless into feeling peaceful wherever we are. It is the strength we have to look within and without when things are imperfect and to adjust our sails whenever necessary. It is often something we develop alone from our own internal suffering, and yet we can also develop our resilience from a sense of connection with others.

The Magic of Resilience

To find lasting success requires that we get in touch with and embrace our inner warrior—our resilience. Resilience is our ability to pull something from deep within to continue moving forward while being tested. And that "thing" we pull from is hope. Hope is what funds our resilience. Resilience is what we use to keep us from quitting. Resilience is the hard work, the sweat, the tears, and our ability to adapt to unpredictable circumstances in order to rise above them. Resilience requires that we have something to believe in. Without something to believe in, it is difficult to stay steadfast in our pursuit. This is where hope comes in. To be resilient, we need hope. When we lose hope, we lose resilience. Hope and resilience go hand in hand. Hope is perhaps the most enchanted emotion. Hope reminds us of our dream, of why we started and why we are still going. It holds the space for all the things we have not yet accomplished. It holds the pearl inside the clam. It keeps us driving and grinding to achieve our dreams.

In reality, we must believe that absolutely nothing we set out to do is insurmountable. This belief drives our resiliency to never give up. We must hold the deep belief that *when there is a will, there is a way.* Resilience is that inexpressible quality that allows us to get knocked down by life and to come back stronger than before. Rather than letting failure overcome us and drain us of our resolve, we find a way to rise from the ashes. Even after misfortune, we are resilient enough to be blessed with an outlook that we are more than able to change course and soldier on.

Coachable Moment

Indeed, this life is a test. It is a test of many things—of our convictions and priorities, our faith and our faithfulness, our patience and our resilience, and in the end, our ultimate desires.

—Sheri L. Dew

The journey will be unpredictable for all of us, but that's part of the excitement of succeeding. Whenever things aren't fully under our control, we are brought again and again into our own self-discovery to grow ourselves to our next level. It is normal to get down on ourselves when we're being challenged. But the struggles we face in life and business are essential to our success. It is out of our suffering that we gain our depth, resilience, and wisdom. We come to find the true meaning behind who we are. Challenge is the gateway to our personal and professional transcendence. Self-discovery leads to clarity. We are able to uncover, acknowledge and properly own our blind spots. We learn to remove barriers to ourselves by challenging old beliefs and analyzing the false assumptions we may hold. We come to see that we don't need to *change* ourselves—we need to *enhance* ourselves.

Character Traits of the Exceptionally Resilient

We grow the most when we suffer. The Bible says that our faith is tried in "the fire of affliction." For this reason, we must not wish our troubles away but work to surpass them. We have to quit telling ourselves that what we're going through is too much. Such defeatist thoughts drain us of our strength and energy. We must come to trust we wouldn't be in the situation we are in if we couldn't handle it. Instead we are equal to it; the obstacle is not bigger than we are. When we suffer, we grow in confidence and strengthen our levels of self-respect. We must not avoid or run from our suffering; rather, we must dig in and experience what it feels like to be down and to rise again. We place the highest honor on our own personal value when we don't give up.

Through our suffering, we learn to self-soothe and are able to operate with a sense of composure regardless of our circumstances. Suffering teaches us where the places are within us that help us survive. It gets us in touch with our will, motivation, and the pliability to change direction if necessary. We come to a place where we carry a natural attitude of faith that all things will work out in our favor because we deeply believe in the value and worth of who we are, what we have to offer, what our goals are, and the importance of our overall life purpose.

Part of developing our resiliency is to allow risk to inspire us, not frighten us. We must be thankful for each risk we take, because each one expands us that much more as a person. Risk is for the resilient, and it makes us less afraid of failure. Because of risk, we come to learn that the joy we feel isn't in the destination but rather in the free fall of the unknown. Joy sprouts from the trial and error, the uncertainty, the evasive outcomes, the late nights, the excitement, the anticipation, and the curiosity of how we can better perfect what we're doing to hit our mark. The joy is in the process of two steps forward, one step back. It is in the working-through process of things. The joy comes in never giving up.

The more resiliency we develop, the more elegantly we move through life. Why? Because we can trust ourselves and our communities to make it through whatever adversity is placed in front of us. We become clear that those who are the loudest tend to be the weakest. The more our character is tested, the more value we see in the less-is-more concept. We do not want what is obnoxious about us, such as our insecurity or needs for attention and acknowledgment, to be the defining traits that make us stand out. The more we flaunt how great we are, the more negative attention we draw to ourselves.

One night on Twitter, I saw that a young aspiring college sports reporter was getting annihilated in social media for taking a selfie of her cleavage with someone else's blood on it during the worst mass murder in United States history at the Route 91 Concert in Las Vegas. Her caption read, "I'm okay. The blood is from helping others. There are many who are not okay. Please, please, please send prayers." People were appalled at how tone deaf her timing was to use a mass murder as an opportunity to take a selfie. She was social media savvy enough to equip her post with all the proper hashtags to get as noticed as possible by TV stations and other such media outlets. This was her chance to get noticed as some kind of hero and hit it big. She definitely got noticed, but not in any way that would help her career or reputation or to build her clearly inflated but fragile sense of self. She was credited for creating a whole new genre of selfies: the mass murder selfie.

Is this how a hero would respond in a traumatic or adverse situation? A real hero would be so consumed with helping others that time to snap a selfie would not have been a thought or a consideration, let alone to also take the time to properly hashtag and post it on social media. A hero would have had more respect for the victims of this tragedy than to use it for self-promotion.

In this world of social media, we must strive to be self-aware, not self-preoccupied. We must come to trust that our hard work, talents, and good character will eventually be recognized and utilized. We must desire to be acknowledged by others for the depth of our will, for the integrity of our actions, and for never giving up in the face of all the hard work and patience it takes to live our dreams.

If we want to be blessed with miracles, we must never search for fame or riches. Instead we must search to make a difference. Fame, like money, will come and go, but having a positive and lasting impact on others lasts long after we are gone. Modesty, humility, compassion, and a giving nature touch hearts. Is there anything more impactful than to be acknowledged for that?

Coachable Moment

Always do your best. What you plant now, you will harvest later.

—Og Mandino

The greatest gift you give to others is to be a really good human being.

An exceptional person living an exceptional life is one who feels deeply, loves fiercely, and is willing to work tirelessly.

Embrace your human emotions, allow them to come, but do not let them hold you back from your goals.

The best way to stand out is to be humble and generous. Be authentic and show you are constantly working on developing your character. Hold the belief that you can learn from everyone.

Leadership

People Skills + Resilience = LEADERSHIP

The first person we must govern well is ourselves.

Anguish is essential for our success, so we must not fret when we suffer. Suffering is essential to the growth of our knowledge, the building of our character, our resiliency, and our empathy.

To be exceptional, to strive beyond the mere striving for success, we must be humble. When leading others, we must be willing to take ownership of our mistakes and utilize them as teachable opportunities. When we admit to our imperfections, we make it okay for others to waver in theirs as well. In doing this, we have the opportunity to empower other people to see themselves, not as deficient but as different. We learn so much from our differences and can utilize these to create a community of people that creates a beautiful and supportive whole. To be great leaders, we must understand that it is the more understated qualities of our character that make us real, approachable, empathetic, hardy, and successful.

To lead well, we must hold high expectations of ourselves and a deep concern for our community. We must consistently acknowledge the responsibility we have to those who love and support us. When our personal values are communicated with open compassion, are put into action, and shared with those in our network, they provide the unity necessary to accomplish any task, goal, or mission. It is our vision that establishes the destination, but it really comes down to mutually shared goals and values we nurture within our community that determine the outcome of our success and happiness.

As leaders, we must remain coachable by keeping our ego in check. Our role as the leader is to stay focused on the dream, the bigger picture, so our team can focus on the details that will lead us to victory.

The most powerful force in success isn't greed, fear, or even the raw energy of unrestrained competition. The most powerful force in success is *caring*. We do not want to be competitive with our own team members. To lead well, we must know ourselves well. Our suffering should shift our focus to something greater than ourselves when we have nowhere to turn. We must come from a strong sense of family and values and have a dedication to some sort of spiritual faith.

We must remain humble to the knowledge that leaders also need leaders. There is no stronger way to be led than to have a power larger than oneself to support and guide us unconditionally. One thing all great leaders have in common is a strong sense of faith. The particular dogma may not be the same, but there is a higher power. Exceptional leaders understand this, which is why they are spiritual.

MARINATE ON THIS

I pray every night, sometimes long prayers about a lot of things and a lot of people, but I don't talk about it or brag about it because that's between God and me, and I'm no better than anybody else in God's sight.

—Petyon Manning

Part 5
SELF-ACTUALIZATION NEEDS

What a man can be, he must be. This need we call Self-Actualization.
—Abraham Maslow

Once the first four levels of physiological, safety, love and belonging, and self-esteem needs are met, Maslow believed we are capable of achieving our true potential. We become human beings who desire to embody truth, seek the deeper meanings in life, and live with wisdom and justice in our every word, deed, and action. Self-actualization moves us to a higher plateau of understanding as well as a greater awareness for the needs of others. It is estimated that only 2 percent of the population achieve this elite level of extraordinary existence, and those of us who do, experience a greater strength of character. We live with a deeper sense of humility and respect for life, others, and ourselves. We have a more natural and instinctual ability to differentiate between the real and the fake. We have come to deeply love, seek, acknowledge, and appreciate the worth of those in our community rather than living solely focused on our status, wealth, or gain. We are more introspective and global in our thought process. We have come to a place where we appreciate the depth and spiritual connectedness with which our suffering has gifted us. We never lose sight of the importance of human needs and emotions.

Suffering + Spirituality = Emotionally Wealthy

There are only two ways to live your life. One is as though nothing is a miracle. The other is as though everything is a miracle.

—Albert Einstein

What is emotional wealth? Emotional wealth means we are physically well, emotionally balanced, mentally healthy, financially well-off, and spiritually well. We have it all. The reasons we use the equations we have examined in this book is to get to this place of emotional wealth, wealthy living. When we are emotionally full and mentally well, we are wealthy. To be rich is one thing, and it is a great thing, but riches only bring money. Having money without all the other elements that matter in life is a terrifying state of misery.

Happiness is a culmination of all the success equations lived consistently. It is about living deeply, living with vulnerability, refusing to take no for an answer, as well as failing, hurting, working hard, and rising.

Wealth is an emotional state. It is not about numbers in the bank. Our bank accounts are only one element that help support us in being emotionally wealthy.

203

The point of life is to feel whole. We are here to find ourselves and to experience being all we can be, do, have, give, and experience. We are here to actualize ourselves to our further-most reaching potentials. The healthier and more well-rounded we become, the more focused we become on *potential* rather than *achievement.* We come to value effort as a more powerful force than either genius or talent. We cannot experience our depths when life comes easy. Emotional wealth is the experience of our ability to get up again and again. It is the feeling that comes when we turn our terrors to triumphs. It is the suffering that brings us to our knees that leads us to the edges of our potential.

When on our knees, we find the humility to seek help from something bigger than ourselves. We find God. It is often when we have no other choices available that we begin to pray. This is where, most especially, that we begin to actualize and start to thrive.

Suffering

SUFFERING + Spirituality = Emotionally Wealthy

All worthy growth develops from necessary levels of despair. We never grow more than when we are questioning everyone and everything and wondering if it's all worth it. When we hurt, we question love, life, faith, God, ourselves, and our reasons to keep going. This is all part of the journey, and it's all necessary. There are more gifts to come from our harder times in life than anything else because nothing stretches us more than to hurt deeply enough to start on the path of asking the deeper reasons of our existence. Our deeper heartbreaks are the windows into ourselves.

Great Life Lessons from Anguish and Stress

There is nothing more trying than carrying a load of stress that feels far beyond our ability to manage. It feels debilitating. When we're panicking, it is nearly impossible to find workable or well thought-out solutions to our problems. Feelings of stress are among the most frightening and powerful emotions we experience along our journey toward success. Both life and business are full of unfair situations, poor communication, deals gone bad, lies told, people underperforming, entitlement expectations, loss of finances, bullies, toxic people, and other let downs. When we're in these stressful times, it is normal to feel out of control, hurt, self-doubt, extreme sadness, anxiety, and fear, coupled with feelings of powerlessness, to change our circumstances. Yet, without these types of stressors, unfair situations, and less than honest or stellar people on our paths, we would never grow into the powerful people we are destined to become.

As beneficial as such situations can be, I don't suggest that we seek them out. They will find us. And as for those people who manage to break us, I urge that we never go back to them. If people do things once, they will do it again. Follow the rule: Betray me once, shame on you; betray me twice, shame on me. Learn when to cut ties and move on to something bigger, better, and worthy of your time and effort. Let each person who betrays you teach you where your boundaries and limits need to be in place. Let these experiences help you conceptualize where other people stop and you start. When you have the feeling that your limits are being manipulated or crossed, you must set clear boundaries or risk being manipulated repeatedly. Not all people are good people, no matter how great or genuine they present themselves to be.

It is a guarantee that, along our journey, we will lose deals, connections, friendships, and even deep loves we had hoped would assist in taking us to our next level. We may have found that many of these opportunities were more false than real, which makes it easy to get down on ourselves and feel a hopeless sense of frustration. Whatever opportunities are lost or taken away, leaving gaping voids in our lives and businesses, will initially be filled with our feelings of stress and heartbreak. However, by design, whatever falls empty will soon become full again.

Coachable Moment

Make an empty space in any corner of your mind, and creativity will instantly fill it.

—Dee Hock

In each experience where we realize we've been manipulated, the awareness we gain is our greatest education. We become attuned to what manipulation looks like and feels like, allowing us to move forward with more wisdom and less wasted time and effort. We all have our softhearted spaces and want to believe this world is full of genuine, loving, and fair people. The reality is that this is not true. Most people, especially in business, are in it solely to gain something for themselves. There is no greater way to develop the wisdom of where our boundaries need to be than through being taken advantage of. We must learn not to repeat the same mistakes over and over again with the same people.

The amazing thing about any heartbreak is that when we give it the time and attention it deserves, it will heal. When we are hurting or things aren't turning around as quickly as we would like, we can come to falsely believe things will never again turn in our favor. This is natural. However, if we allow ourselves to get stuck here, this type of thinking becomes defeatist and nonproductive. Time heals. This we can trust. Stress and hardship, although not enjoyable, do pass, and as time moves on, solutions come. In the meantime, we must make sure to focus on working hard and finding a level of acceptance for the situation we are in. All uncertainties settle and work themselves out—maybe not in the vision we had originally held, but many times things often take on an even brighter opportunity.

Coachable Moment
Pain will come, and the great news is ... *pain will end*!
—*Dr. Sherrie Campbell*

Stress and adversity are extremely painful. No one ever promised life would be fair, but if we can hold tight to faith, keep moving forward, and continue working hard, what was lost or meant for our harm will soon turn in our favor. When we're stressed or heartbroken, we must focus even more intently on keeping our eyes on the prize. These are the times we will want to give up the most, when in reality these are times we need to work our hearts out and stay focused. When we make the choice to keep moving forward, we won't have to wait to see the light at the end of the tunnel. Instead we will *create* the light that will expel our darkness.

It takes a tremendous amount of courage to go toe-to-toe with our heartbreak. And no matter how debilitating these times feel, it doesn't mean that they actually are. We can overcome them, but we need courage to do so. And courage isn't something we have. It is something we do. How do we become courageous? By doing courageous things. Courage is like a muscle: the more we use it, the stronger it gets. The only way to get rid of our fears is to do the things we fear, face the things we'd rather avoid, and keep moving forward when our impulses are pressuring us to freeze. If we allow ourselves to stay blocked or stuck, we cannot grow and our situation has no potential for change.

Coachable Moment

I learned that courage was not the absence of fear, but the triumph over it. The brave man is not he who does not feel afraid, but he who conquers that fear.

—*Nelson Mandela*

The only way things in our lives or circumstances change is when we change. Adversity will change us in our core because all change, especially unwanted change, forces us to either grow or stop. We are creatures of habit, and most of us naturally prefer a certain amount of familiarity and predictability to our lives. Adversity teaches us to have the faith that if something in our life or career changes or even ends, it is because it wasn't working properly. Throughout our lives and careers, there will be situations that won't get better, but that doesn't mean *we* can't get better.

We get better as we learn to let go of what we cannot control and adapt to what is new. Surrender is an essential ingredient to moving through any type of stress or heartbreak. Surrendering to things as they are is the greatest risk we take, but it is only through doing this that the space for change or healing is created. Being rigid, stubborn, or unmoving blocks opportunities, creativity, new solutions, and the exact answers we may be looking for. We must recognize that *surrendering to what is* takes incredible courage. We can all survive the scarier times in life. Adversity teaches us that we are 100 percent capable of surviving even when we think we can't or won't.

I believe that when you have no other choice but to move on, you will, and you will come out stronger and more successful because of the experience. Nothing teaches you more about getting through your self-doubts than forcing yourself to get through them. Through each loss, you gain understanding. You are never more malleable than when you are feeling defeated and in need of help, structure, or guidance. As you grow through these unpleasant times, you come to understand when a new opportunity walks into your life and why things didn't work out for you in the first place or with the people you were with before.

Experiences with defeat or loss not only build our resilience but also refine us into being better human beings. Stress provides, with optimal levels of frustration, that which helps us cope with new demands and expectations. Life will consistently provoke us to grow. And life's stresses make us move and make our lives worth living. It is our painful feelings that awaken us to discover who we are and how deeply and intensely we have the capacity to *feel.*

You will learn to rise through your tests and trials. I can guarantee you this as a psychologist. The confusing part about passing through loss is that even though you intellectually know it will pass, when you're in the throws of it, it feels as if it is never going to shift or change in your favor. Uncertainty is a painful journey. It's a journey that you will undertake many times over in your lifetime, in many different areas of your life, and for many different reasons. You may as well buckle up and accept that the journey through your stress and heartbreak serve as the character building devices you need in an effort to take full accountability for yourself, your life, your life-trajectory, and the intelligent management of your emotions. Without suffering, you cannot develop wisdom. Heartbreaks sustain and define the depth and richness of your character. They will make you stronger, more mindful, and elegant in your approach to love, life, and business.

Staying Inspired through Times of Suffering

To be successful to the levels we desire, we must have joy. Success without joy is not success at all. We must feel excited to wake up each morning to do what we love to do. Every day isn't going to be perfect, and there are tedious things about our career we won't like, but the bigger picture of what we do is what makes the effort so worth it. To be an entrepreneur puts us into a unique group of people—a group in which we desire to be set apart from being average. We are driven from deep in our soul for something more meaningful, exciting, and significant. We tend *not* to be those who follow the crowd. We live with deep levels of desire, a strong sense of independence, needs for creative freedom, bottomless levels of dedication, and the fearlessness to be different and take risks.

Staying inspired can be difficult, however, so I would like to pass along to you some great strategies that can help you remain inspired. First, be obsessed with your own *personal enhancement*. We must nurture our mind, commit to being bookworms, and surround ourselves with motivational information. One of my personal favorites is the *Motivation Manifesto*, by Brendan Burchard. I can read one sentence from this book and the entire trajectory of my mind-set is fundamentally changed. It is so inspiring to read the exact words I need to hear that instantly connect me to why I am doing what I am doing and the reasons I am working so hard to do it. What I read in this book inspires me to reach deeper, to want more, and to live my life experiences more fully. It simply amazes me how words placed together in perfect sequence can touch my heart so deeply—deeply enough to inspire my passions into action. Reading something that hits home reminds us that our path to success is worth the hard work. Having a book on hand is like having a pocket coach. When we need it, we can reach for it at a moment's notice.

Second, getting *time alone* is central to staying creative and inspired. We spend the majority of our time in the company of other people. Even when the connections we have are positive, it is still taxing on our energy to be constantly giving out. It is necessary for our spirits to have a certain amount of time alone to detox and re-energize. Inspiration cannot come from a dry well of energy resources. We must take the necessary time to recharge and reboot our energy systems. This is the freedom we all need. Sometimes there is nothing more creative than being in our own energy, exploring our thoughts and ideas without the influence of others. We need time to reconnect and get back to ourselves. We cannot neglect ourselves and expect to have a consistent flow of inspired energy.

Third, as leaders and entrepreneurs, *making more money* is an effective strategy for inspiring us to work hard. Success feels great, and money is an important part of the picture we hold of success. Money is a great motivator, not the root of all evil. We must view money as a great tool and resource that can be used for so much good. Money is also one of the greatest rewards acknowledging our hard work. It is not wrong to work for money or to have making more money as a priority and important goal in our lives. We must remove the "guilt" around money. It's not bad to have it and to have a lot of it. And having it and earning it are not signs of greed. Increases in money often come hand-in-hand with increases in our status and position, all of which build our confidence and reputation. With money comes the freedom to do more things. Having this type of freedom contributes to our feeling more happiness, worth, and overall satisfaction. It is also true that to be solely driven for money will not bring much success, or at least not the type of success that lasts, so it is important to have a healthy relationship with money where it is respected rather than worshiped. Money is something we earn and also something we give—giving being one of the greatest success strategies we can utilize.

Fourth, we must have a tremendous amount of *faith*. As we climb through our journey, we will all face times of feeling as if things are moving too slowly or that we are not getting where we want to go in the ways that we had hoped or envisioned. Such is life. The stress of all the navigating and problem-solving we must undertake can make life feel extremely taxing. So to stay inspired or to even rediscover our inspiration, we have to make use of all of our senses to help us learn to wait well, to have the faith in ourselves and in our higher power that we will succeed.

Fifth, in the success equation about *exercise*, we talked about how getting outside, moving our body, getting fresh air, and working up a sweat are highly creative ways to find inspiration. When we are at work, our mind is only focused on the task at hand, which leaves very little room for our right-brained activities, such as inspiration, to come forth. When we exercise, the left brain is distracted by the task of exercising, allowing our right-brained emotions and ideas to come through. Further, when we push ourselves physically, we learn how strong we are emotionally, and this helps keep us inspired and believing in our capacities to continue pressing forward. I can say that when I run, the most creative ideas I have for my business come to mind, so much so that I bring an audio recorder with me to document them.

⎯⎯⎯

Coachable Moment

(a note I wrote to running one day after I was outside on the trails)

Dear Running,

I want to thank you for the following:

When I feel weak, you remind me that I am strong. When I feel sad, you magically lift me to a higher level of consciousness where I can see the bigger purpose of what is happening. When I feel like I can't push myself any further, you remind me of the grit I have within to thrive forward. When I feel void of answers, you provide them to me. When I feel lost to my creativity, you graciously flood my mind with ideas. When I feel like I can't take any more, you remind me I have it in me to stand on my own. When I feel like breaking down, you show me I have what it takes to go on. When I push myself physically, I am reminded of how strong I am emotionally. You hold my conversations with God. I am always reminded of my direction as you teach me that answers I need are within me. I consider you amongst the most important relationships in my life. You are always there for me without fail to nurture me. What I learn from you, I cannot get in any other way. For these reasons …

I love you.

When I run, it brings me back to my original vision of success and fulfillment.

Sixth, when we lose the feeling of being inspired, it is a great strategy *to go back to the drawing board* and either revisit the vision of what it is that we want or be brave and flexible enough to reinvent our vision to move forward more effectively. Having a vision is a way of creating a future benchmark of achievement that sits out luminously in front of us, and we will not be satisfied until we achieve it. A vision inspires the willingness to strive for what we want. It inspires us to live our dream again and again.

Seventh, a sense of *competition* is an incredibly effective strategy to use to stay inspired. Whether we're competing with ourselves, a score, a dollar amount, another person, for a raise or a bonus, or chasing a certain goal, competition breeds inspiration. Competition inspires us to get to that next level. It motivates us to prove ourselves to ourselves and to those others who matter as we're pushing ourselves forward. Getting to that next level will require hard work, training, and motivation. Still, there is nothing more inspiring than wanting to win. We will naturally do nearly anything to feel that sense of accomplishment. Competition can be a beautiful thing.

Finally, if we want to feel the reasons we are doing what we're doing when we forget, we can find that inspiration in the simple act of *giving*. When we give, we see the fruits of our labor. We see the reasons why we're doing what we're doing, and why where we're going matters. Seeing the significance of our impact on the world is so moving that it will absolutely inspire us to work more and earn more in order to have the continual opportunity to give more. Giving is the greatest gift that gives back. Witnessing the gifts of what we contribute to others is one of the most fulfilling parts of being human. We feel good when we make others feel good. It is what inspiration is all about.

Part of the problem with inspiration for many of us who are aspiring or already thriving entrepreneurs is *creating a healthier work-life balance.* Many of us neglect to give enough attention to our physical, mental, or emotional well-being. We get into patterns of working at all hours, we eat whatever is closest to us, and we often blindly finish tasks when under pressured-situations. This type of lifestyle is a recipe for burnout. The state of mind that ignites inspiration becomes more elusive if we aren't addressing our own needs along the way. Whenever we neglect ourselves, we suffer. When we suffer, our feeling of being inspired also suffers. We must use our suffering to garner a depth of understanding within ourselves and in our thoughts about life where we become more inspired than ever to keep going.

When we can find the meaning in our suffering, we understand where true inspiration comes from. We never truly know our own depths and what we're capable of until we hurt beyond what we think we're capable of surviving. When we suffer, we find who we are spiritually. We find something bigger than ourselves to believe in and count on. We find our version of God—t he One who doesn't live in a church, a mosque, a tent, a temple, a teepee, or any other structure but rather lives within our own heart. The only place then that we have to go to access inspiration is within.

Spirituality
Suffering + SPIRITUALITY = Emotionally Wealthy

Spirituality means something different to everyone. For some, it's about participating in organized religion: going to a church, synagogue, mosque, and so on. For others, it's more personal, with some people getting in touch with their spiritual side through private prayer, yoga, meditation, quiet reflection, or even long walks.

Spirituality is a naturally occurring part of us. Our brain processes sensory experiences in such ways that we naturally look for patterns and then seek to uncover the meaning in those patterns. Once we believe in something, we will try to explain away anything that conflicts with it. As human beings, we cannot help but ask big questions; the task is hardwired into our minds to do so.

Suffering Leads to the Depths of Our Spirit

The one thing suffering forces us to do is dig deeply, search, question, reinvent, and start again. When we hurt, we instantly think more deeply. We search for what is sacred, for what can save or help us, for something loving and solid we can grab onto, believe, and count on. Life has terrifying moments. And virtues, such as faith, hope and confidence, abandon us from time to time as we are pulled along through a painful time. Such things destine us to discover the deeper, more existential purpose to our lives. Suffering, after all, is painful enough to grab our attention, to bring us to our knees. It almost always brings us to prayer too. It brings us to the broken parts of ourselves and can help us see our strengths. It brings us to want to understand the reasons things happen as they do. It brings us to God.

Spiritual Tenets to Guide Success

When we believe in something bigger than ourselves and mold our lives around a strong value system, we live feeling grateful and excited for all that this miracle of life has to offer.

The true essence of anything spiritual is simplicity. It's not hard to find a simple formula to live by. Have you ever read the book *All I Really Need to Know I Learned in Kindergarten*, by Robert Fulghum? The points he makes are great examples of the simplicity it takes to make our lives work with a sense of harmony. There is a saying that the truth behind all spiritual beliefs is essentially the same. The more complicated a belief system, the more complicated life becomes. At the core, however, we are all the same. Emotions are the universal language. We all feel them the same way. What triggers the emotions will vary from person to person, but the way they are *felt*, the way they *feel inside*, is the same for all of us. Life really doesn't have to be as complicated as we make it. If we can master what is simple, we can triumph over the insurmountable.

Remember naptime in kindergarten? We were taught we need a little sleep or quiet time in our day, so we have what it takes to be well behaved and rested for the remainder of the day. When we're tired, we're cranky, and kindergarten teachers loved themselves enough to avoid spending their day with unrested, cranky kids. Well, as adults we must not sacrifice this simple practice.

It is also healthy for us to practice some form of *meditation*. When we take some time to ourselves to intentionally commune with our spirit, we feel more alive. How we each find this communion will vary: some individuals meditate, some run, others go to yoga, some read, some spend time in prayer and go to church, some write in their journal, and others nap. It doesn't matter how we meditate; it only matters that we do. The time we spend within is how we connect, refuel, and take up communication with the virtues of hope, love, and faith that are handed to us by God. No matter our stress, in private time of communion we come to trust that if God brought something to us, then God will bring us through it.

How much time we need to connect internally may differ from day to day. Some of us may need to go inward a strict twenty to thirty minutes per day to stay disciplined. We're all different, so we must do what we feel is right is for us. In this time to bond within ourselves, we must practice letting down our judgments of ourselves and others. We must use it as a well-deserved break from the chaos or our racing critical mind. It's a time to let go of what is happening in the outside world, be in our own space, and create a calm, cool space for us to relax into. We are better able to connect with the Source of our passion when we take the time to do so. It allows us to let go of our fears, putting us back in touch with the power we have to be our own miracle maker.

When we are connected within, we are better at *sharing*. When we are depleted, we are grabbing at everything and anything to be ours in case we lose it. We must remind ourselves of how simple it is to share and how beneficial this simple practice is in living a healthy, happy, and fulfilling life. We cannot succeed in any form if we do not know how to practice giving and receiving. And giving is easy. It feels great to give and have the resources available to do so. On the other hand, it is amazing how many of us feel guilty or uncomfortable when we receive. God desires to show us his love through what others desire to give to us. If we do not feel worthy of receiving, life won't be nearly as fulfilling. The Universe of love, success, and miracles operates through the exchange of giving and receiving. We must give what we seek, and keep an abundance of love and goodness circulating throughout every aspect of our life. We must know our value and be thankful that others see it and desire to acknowledge it. In kindergarten, we learn to share and be kind. We don't have to give gifts everywhere we go, just loving-kindness.

I blog every day on Facebook to well over 65,000 followers. I blog from personal experience, from what I live, love, read, and am learning or have learned. I do this every day, and I do it for free. I do it because I love people, and I want to share what I have learned from my own suffering. Because of this, a woman on my page voted for me to win a Beauty In Beauty Out Award in 2015 in the state of California. Fifteen women win this award each year. When I was notified of this honor, I didn't think it was real. I didn't think I could win anything like this for blogging. The night I won the award, gave my speech, and had my chosen loves living in this moment with me, I experienced firsthand how what I was doing daily was saving lives, helping people through divorces, deaths, illnesses, heartbreaks, and learning to love themselves better through setting healthier boundaries. I truly believe I get way more from this page than I believe I could ever give. I believe my purpose on this planet is to love, help, and educate others, to help them turn their own pain to the positive. The opportunities and recognition that come from my Facebook page continue to astound me. They are the side effect of doing something I love to do.

We must make it a conscious effort each day that wherever we go and whomever we encounter, we bring *kindness* along with us. It's so easy to be kind, while it takes so much negative energy and mental planning to be manipulative and angry. We must give kindness, in some form, to everyone we encounter. We must look for the good and point out the good that we see in others. We must tell people why they matter. As we circulate this type of joy, wealth, and love into the lives of others, it will come back to us tenfold. On the other hand, if this is done manipulatively, selfishly, or only to receive, it will not work. This Universe only responds to what is genuine. The most valuable gifts we can give are affection, appreciation, caring, compassion, empathy, and love. Each time we meet another person, we must silently wish for him or her to have joy, happiness, and fulfillment. We must live wisely to the knowledge that every action has an equal reaction. We must think about the laws of cause and effect as we live our lives, if we are to be the type of person we want to be.

We must be mindful of who we are and what we're seeking. We must be careful not to get power mixed up with control or love. Every action we put into this world generates a force of energy that returns to us like a boomerang. The Bible makes it clear that we reap what we sow. When we choose actions that bring happiness and success to others, the fruit of our karma is happiness and success. For this reason, *be a good human*. It's that simple. Whatever choices we make, we should make mindfully. The way for any of us to prosper in any given moment is to be conscious of who we are and genuine in our intention to support our actions. We must live with forethought and try to predict what the consequences of our actions and decisions may be. This does not mean we cannot be assertive, firm, or direct, or that we must live paranoid. It means that whatever we do, we do it honestly. Sometimes telling people the hard truth is the most loving thing we can do for them. We must do all we can to direct our choices to benefit, not just ourselves, but as many others as possible.

If we don't know what choices to make, we can ask our heart for guidance, trust our *intuition*, and do what we think is best. We will face many uncertain choices and outcomes. All we can do is do our best. The more we follow our inner visions, the better the decisions we learn to make. Life is hardly ever going to be fully certain for us, so we must leap with abandon and good intentions, and trust we will land in the right place. Our inner visions are God-given, so we must act on them. The unexpected is an essential part of our spiritual development. Working smarter comes down to decision-making. When we make the correct decisions, we can focus on movement forward rather than cleaning up the mess we made. Every decision we make, good and bad, helps us glean knowledge we can trust. These are the gifts of life's playbook of lessons. As we come to trust our knowledge, we are able to live with more acceptance—accepting people, circumstances, situations, and events as they occur. When we do this, we are better able to roll with the unexpected curves.

The great spiritualist Lao Tzu says, "Do by not doing and it will all get done." When we have given all of our time, effort, thought, and energy to something and we still don't get the result we want, sometimes the best thing to do is to accept that we may not get our desired result. There is a time, when all avenues have been exhausted, to stop all the doing by giving things the space and time to settle. The beautiful thing about *acceptance* is that once we accept life on its terms, it relieves our heartbreak. Once we have acceptance, we can move into action and take responsibility for where we are. Now, we can make changes, but we stop the blame-game, which includes blaming ourselves. We must come to view our challenges as opportunities dressed in disguise. Acceptance is a form of openness. When we accept something fully, we relinquish our need to defend our point of view and feel no need to persuade others to accept what we think. Instead, we remain open to all points of view without rigidly attaching to any of them until we find the one that fits our situation and desired directions best. This is what it means to allow the winds of heaven to blow through our lives. Acceptance provides a letdown of ego and creates space for the miracle.

As we operate in these more open and effective ways, we start to feel freedom from the heartbreak. We lift ourselves out of terror and back into being the people we need to be to get up and keep on going. Life's greatest gift is that we can always start again. Life has an unlimited supply of starts. We must start with renewed intentions and desires. Intrinsic to every intention and desire we hold are the mechanics for their fulfillment. As soon as we have an intention, we activate our potential to fulfill what we want with organization and strategy. We have the inbuilt mechanics to fulfill every intention, desire, and potential we can muster. The organizing power to accomplish our dreams is birthed instantaneously with the clarity of our intention. For this reason, we should be continually making lists of all things we desire to experience and do this without casting judgment on ourselves or on others. We should keep this list on hand at all times.

We must make it our intention to nurture the uniqueness of who we are and to love ourselves so we can better serve other people. We must awaken to this each morning to live from our God-Self. To be good to ourselves and to others, to do our best, be our best, and give our best to the best of our ability. We must walk in the truth and allow ourselves room for human error no matter how hard or disappointing that may be. Most importantly, we must help and allow others to do the same. We must ask ourselves, *How can I serve?* and *How can I help?* The answers to these questions are what help us to be *good humans*. Good humans are the types of leaders we need in today's society.

⚶

Coachable Moment

You can't connect the dots looking forward; you can only connect them looking backwards. So, you have to trust that the dots will somehow connect in your future. You have to trust in something—your gut, destiny, life, karma, whatever. This approach has never let me down, and it has made all the difference in my life.

—Steve Jobs

The Spiritual Way of Leading Our Lives with Compassion

We each have the potential to be the emotional leaders and nurturers of the world.

The emotions are what connect all of us, what unite us. We are each leaders in our own right, and each of us will lead with our own unique style, but the one trait we must all call upon to be great leaders is compassion. By placing ourselves in the shoes of another, by feeling what another is feeling, we have the power to move people out of their heads and place them in their hearts.

To do this, we must continually cultivate our self-awareness, another tenant from one of the first equations. To lead from our heart, we must be deeply knowledgeable about ourselves and committed to our own personal development. We must trust that the only way to lead another is to be the great leader of our own life. We can only lead another as far as we have gone ourselves. We must have the courage to lead with our truth and the telling of our own story because it is the life experience we've had that is our most powerful influence.

Compassion is developed through life's hard knocks. It comes from our ability to rise, knowing how very hard rising again often is. We know that we would never want to follow leaders who had never suffered because they would not know what to do on the frontlines of a hardship. For this reason, we must be deeply thankful for the lessons our heartbreaks have taught us.

We can use compassion to heal nearly all miscommunications. If we have the knowledge that love and understanding are transformational, we can bring this open quality into our conversations and move people from feeling stuck into feeling a sense of hope again. When consideration isn't present, solutions are one-sided rather than reciprocal. When consideration is present, communication becomes a two-way, collaborative, fair, and reflective process. It allows for vulnerability and for all involved to feel seen and important. The most important thing we can do when we communicate is meet people exactly where they are. We must train ourselves to think of others before ourselves whenever necessary. One of the greatest spiritual tenets we must live by is to treat others the way we would want to be treated. When we love ourselves, we have a lot of love and guidance to give. When we love ourselves, we move from being people-haters into being lovers of humans.

The Joy of an Awakened Spirit

Work is work.

Money is great.

But we must be careful not to get caught up in worshiping the God of Green Paper.

Money provides the gift of having the freedom to do more and have more, but what it doesn't provide is love or happiness. In fact, money without love is a deeply experienced misery. We can have it all and still feel vastly empty.

Happiness is not a product of money but a byproduct of achievement. Happiness is best gained when we're working from something and for something larger than ourselves.

The experience of succeeding ultimately comes when we have the capacity to share our success, all that we have learned and gained. Sharing gives us a deeper and more meaningful experience of ourselves, money, success, life, and people. For this reason, we must have some connection to a philosophy of life that is bigger than solely feeding our egos and our material desires. The more spiritual we are, the more connected we are to something beyond the daily grind of our humanness, the more we enjoy and appreciate the success we've gained through contributing to others in ways that we see make a meaningful difference. This is the joy that comes from an awakened heart.

An awakened heart represents our ability to love. As we grow in our ability to love, we increase our capacity to feel the pain and joy we share with others. The protective walls made up of our opinions, judgments, and barriers start to come down. When we have an awakened heart, we live with less fear. Where fear once was, an opening is created. We are more open to seizing our vulnerable moments because we understand the undeniable depth of their teachings. In seizing our vulnerable moments, we open up to the lessons that come from our times of loneliness. We open up to the depths of our feelings of love and gratitude. We can even find the growth opportunities in our moments of embarrassment or inadequacy. When we have an awakened heart, we more easily accept ourselves and others as wholly and perfectly human.

When we work from the joy of an awakened heart, we see increases in the following areas.

Quality of life

Our life is improved by the idea that we're not alone. The majority of spiritual traditions provide consistent participation in a community of people who embrace and welcome our presence. Whether that comes through attending a church or synagogue, a meditation group, a yoga studio, or a Spartan race team, such groups provide a sense of belonging and serve as a strong network of social and emotional support. Feeling we belong somewhere, to some form of dogma or to a meaningful life philosophy, brings us a sense of safety and security. These types of strong bonds increase our feelings of well-being. They bring our expectations about life and relationships and our ideas of success into a more clear and meaningful perspective. They give us not only a place to receive but also a place to serve and to contribute our knowledge and resources.

Support through challenge

When we feel spiritually connected to a group of similar people, we have more strength to overcome our harder times in life. The spiritual tenets we follow serve as the platform for our personal growth and development. As we get stronger, we come to view our painful times as contemplative opportunities, and eventually come to trust that the hardships we pass through are designed to make us stronger and wiser. When we have a strong sense of community, our faith deepens around the idea that we are internally and externally supported to come out on top. Our community provides us the refuge and resiliency we need when we need them the most.

Interconnectedness

Spirituality helps us identify with and recognize the interconnectedness of our lives with all other things and people. When our heart breaks and we're moving through the gut-wrenching process of grief, having a sense of God helps us frame our experiences as passages that many have taken before us. Knowing that others have undergone similar traumas softens the blow; we feel less isolated and alone in our experiences. Mistakes and failures are an important and shared part of the human experience. No one gets out of life pain free. So it is important to practice self-compassion—to love ourselves regardless of our mistakes or failures.

The beauty of a spiritual philosophy is that it never abandons us; it upholds us. When we learn we are not *by* ourselves, we realize how much we are *with* ourselves.

Mindful choices

The more we love ourselves and respect our lives and other people, the healthier the choices we make in nearly every area of life. Spirituality is about being loving, healthy, humble, and kind. Therefore, when we adhere to this perspective, we tend to treat our body with more kindness, and tend to avoid making unhealthy choices physically, emotionally, relationally, and financially. Spiritual tenets keep us mindful not to drink too much, not to be violent or unkind, and to engage in behaviors that are life-preserving for ourselves and others. When we make choices from the goodness and integrity within us, we live with more peace and maturity.

Acceptance of life

Having an acceptance of life and people is good medicine. When we practice acceptance, we stop expecting life to be easy and pain free. We start living life on life's terms. We are able to accept people for who they are, and we let go of needing them to be different.

We also come to trust that some people cannot be a healthy part of our lives. We need to keep our lives clean of toxicity. The less toxic our lives, the more room we create for our own success and happiness.

As we learn to set healthier boundaries, we are better able to forgive and gain some control over our urges to blame and hold onto hurt feelings. Living this way lowers our blood pressure, helping us live more vibrantly. The less we harbor bitterness, anger, and hurt, the better our heart-health.

Spiritual conversation

We must have conversations with (our idea of) God daily. The form of this conversation doesn't matter, but having it does. This conversation is the direct connection we have to ourselves, to the inner us that holds a wisdom that rises far above all of our worries and fears. When we have these conversations, it feels as if we've been taken from the basement of our emotional house, where we are in the dark and without insight, and lifted to the fifth floor where we can see things from a higher, more evolved perspective. We go from being totally limbic to having the clarity of the prefrontal cortex where rational thought can guide us. Life is always more positive when we're not stuck in our primal reactions. Our internal spiritual conversations keep us in touch with ourselves and the bigger picture of our lives.

Humility

Conceit is self-given. It is molded around money, power, and control. If we worship the God of Green Paper, we will live with an underground relentless fear that any or all of our material possessions, including our income, can be taken away at any time and without our consent. For this reason, we must never worship the material or boast about our power.

When we have a spiritual philosophy, we are more generous, we give credit to others, we involve ourselves in charities, and we commit to random acts of kindness. Most importantly, we do all of this quietly—not to advertise how great we are in an effort to gain attention. Spirituality keeps us humble. We come to understand that the more we give, the more we listen, offer empathy, and take time for others—in other words, the wealthier we feel. If we're going to be wealthy in this life, money is certainly an important part of that equation, but love must come first for us to have the emotional wealth to sustain our spirits.

Spirituality helps to buffer our fears, to protect our hearts, and to bring us a sense of resilience as provided from a spiritual community. A strong life philosophy raises our level of consciousness. We become more thoughtful and patient in how we handle ourselves, how we handle others, and how we think about life and approach our problems. Spirituality brings a depth and maturity that develops us into healthier, happier, and wealthier people.

Spirituality is forever, whereas money comes and goes. For this reason, don't strive for financial success alone. Strive to experience the depths of what it means to be an *emotionally wealthy human being*.

Emotionally Wealthy
Suffering + Spirituality = EMOTIONALLY WEALTHY

To be a true success, we cannot just be rich (money). We must strive for a wealthy life in which we are succeeding in love and relationships, we are physically healthy, mentally strong, emotionally well, and resilient, and we are spiritually connected and financially abundant. Money is only *one* thing, and it is just a *thing*. It may bring riches, but it doesn't bring wealth. Wealth comes from cultivating the more silent virtues that help us live a wholeheartedly and deeply loved life.

So what exactly does it mean to be *emotionally wealthy*?

It means that we have love, friendship, a rich inner life, happiness, friends, free time, and wisdom.

It means we have suffered.

It means we have money and plenty of it, that we are self-aware, and that we love deeply and are treasured and appreciated in return.

When we have emotional wealth, we feel supported. There is a purpose to our lives that expands far beyond us.

If we are emotionally wealthy, we are deeply and truly happy. We radiate from the inside out, and people notice us and the kindness we give. We are available to help others who deserve our love in all the ways that we can.

When we live from the true experience of emotional wealth, we live with more confidence because our emotional wealth has been *earned*. We have grown out of the place of feeling as if we need to audition for the acceptance or approval of others. We no longer live from the insecurity of the "pick me, pick me" attitude. We have become wise as we have grown. We have used our success equations consistently and have triumphed through our heartbreaks. We know life will be difficult and no longer resist this concept. We see the benefits to our personal growth that come from our suffering. And we find that in our suffering we start to develop our personal relationship with God.

Coachable Moment

"Thank you" is the best prayer that anyone could say. I say that one a lot.
Thank you expresses extreme gratitude, humility, understanding.

—*Alice Walker*

When we feel emotionally wealthy, it is indescribable.

Life feels more complete.

We live with a trust, serenity, and inner richness many cannot fathom or comprehend.

We feel human. We embrace feeling human, flaws and all.

We have grown in maturity, in our inner stability, in our faith in life, and in our belief in the magic of the Universe. We have grown from our hard work and from the achievement of our goals. We have grown from all of those people and opportunities lost and gained. We have come to see the perfection in all of it.

We know our personal worth runs much deeper than our income.

We are emotionally wealthy because we have had to cultivate our *resilience*. We can trust the depths of our inner strength. We have come to expect that we will encounter a host of mean, jealous, and cruel people. We now know that this means we're doing something right. We no longer court these types of people for their connection or approval. In fact, these negativities make us even more relentless in our pursuit of happiness and to go out and change the world in any way we can. We know the potential to forever expand upon our success and that the depth of our happiness is the best revenge to have on those who have set themselves up to be a part of our destruction.

Through all of our trials, tribulations, and amazing moments of succeeding, we have found the *Source* of our power. We have developed a loving connection within, and it is from this connection we have learned to live from good intentions. Because we operate from love, we have the possibility to endlessly expand upon our potential. Love is limitless, unlike success. Because we operate from love, it allows us to rise far above the low-level haters. We are well trained not to give our power to anyone or anything that is self-serving, destructive, or manipulative. We have learned to rid our lives of such people, and the most effective way to do this is to take from them what they desire the most—our attention.

When we live with this type of emotional wealth, *we do not give our attention to any meaningless distractions*. We keep our eyes forward. We make no time for blame or criticism. We let go of resentments because they hold us back, keeping us stuck in situations that have long passed. We have come to learn that staying bitter is a complete waste of our energy because there is no depth of our own bitterness that has the power to change what has already happened. We use our success equations to move us upward and onward. If someone else holds resentment against us and will not let go of the grudge, we move on from these people as well. The grudge they hold is not our circus, not our monkey, not our burden.

The more fulfilled we make our lives and the more wholeheartedly we show up to life, *the less willing we are to compromise* who we are and what we believe. When we live by healthy values physically, emotionally, mentally, and spiritually, we have a beautiful and promising platform to stand upon. There is no need to compromise ourselves by living smaller in an effort to make others more comfortable with who they are.

Because we're emotionally wealthy, there will be very few who will really know our income, for we choose to be more *well known for the depth of our character*. We are clear that it takes a small mind to criticize a brilliant one, so we choose to remain unwaveringly true to our life's purpose and to the continuity of our own personal development.

We have developed our emotional wealth through the practice of *living by faith*. We practice choosing faith over fear in our everyday lives. It has been our faith that has brought us through our heartbreaks and strengthened our spirit time and again. Through our suffering, we have come to love ourselves and to understand who we are, and because of this we are unafraid to go after what we want. We will never be immune to having to work through fears and self-doubts because we're human. What we have come to embrace about ourselves is that all that we are and do demonstrate the commitment we have to our purpose here in life. For this reason, we do not fear our journey. We do not fear the deep commitment it takes to live an extraordinary life. We choose to leave a significant impact on the lives of others in the most positive ways we can. We have come to take as much pride in our struggles as our contributions since both are necessary to be emotionally wealthy.

For us, true mastery, lasting success, and deep happiness can only come through *hard work, real sweat, genuine challenge, and surviving life's storms*. We have developed the wherewithal to accept that life is difficult, and because we embrace this truth, we are better able to transcend it. Our success equations have trained us to put responsibility before leisure and to choose kindness over rightness. This is maturity. Maturity and mental health are synonymous. Think about it. Have you ever met an immature, mentally healthy person? We cannot achieve emotional wealth without a deep sense of responsibility.

We have learned, through much painful trial and error, what it means to be *discerning*. We've no doubt been hurt along the way, but we have learned to take responsibility for our heart. We do not expose ourselves to people who discourage or demoralize us. We know we must be deliberate in keeping company with those similar others who are also driven, inspired, honest, and committed to doing something special with their lives. We understand that emotions are contagious and stay clear of those who want to bring us down. We know we're as vulnerable as anyone else, and we remain mindful of this when deciding who stays and who goes in our lives.

We have worked to become *authentic*. Our authenticity keeps us living in truth, making it easier to spot the fake news manipulators. There is no emotional wealth or value in being a loud, one-hit wonder or a greedy, needy chaser of fame and fortune. We are real. We aren't afraid to be vulnerable. We have developed the courage to show the world who we are. We let people in because we know that solid relationships are based in openness, honesty, authenticity, and integrity.

People don't have to guess about who we are and what we are about. Others know exactly where we stand. We expect the absolute best from others because we give the best of ourselves. Giving our very best is exactly what makes us feel so alive.

There is no better feeling in the world than looking forward to waking up each morning *thankful* for another day to chase our dreams. We wake up committed to do our best. We do not take our lives, loves, opportunities, or people for granted. We do not entertain thoughts of laziness. Instead, we feel consumed with an internal sense of urgency and enthusiasm to get ready, to be ready, and to make magic happen. That is what work is for us—it's magic. It's where we can most openly explore, create, and express the intention of our true nature. For this reason, we deeply value our time and the time other people give us.

We have cultivated a deep respect and understanding that we must be *direct* and *committed* to focusing on who and what we love. By focusing on our passions, we figure out what we need to do to continue our growth in those passions.

We are also deeply aware that we will not love every part of our journey. We have learned to *discipline* ourselves to tolerate the more tedious details we dread because we see their value as necessary for us to realize our vision.

That being said, we cannot be healthy or wealthy working 24/7. The sum-total of our success equations has taught us the necessity for *self-compassion* and *preservation*. We make sure to schedule in the necessary time to love ourselves, refuel, and nurture our spirits. We look forward to unplugging from the world of action and excitement. We have come to appreciate the slower moments in life when we have nothing to do but live, rest, meditate, read, exercise, go on vacation, and have fun spending some of the income we have earned. To live with emotional wealth, we must set and respect our limits. We have learned we must say no when we need to because a person without limits is not solid enough to withstand the journey. We count on our inner world and the world of our supportive community to be our sources of power and guidance. We know what is right and what is wrong based in our life experiences. For us, no actually means no.

Saying no is a statement of our *worth*. It is the way we let others know that we will always be, first and foremost, true to ourselves. We have become strong and confident enough to fully embrace who we are. We no longer waste time thinking about fitting in because we are too engrossed in standing out for being *exactly who we are*. Our journey through the life equations has taught us that those individuals who try so hard to fit in are afraid to be themselves. We no longer hold these fears. We know our success has largely come as a result of our uniqueness. It takes great bravery to live according to our own unique compass. In living this way, we can rank ourselves among the greatest mavericks, pioneers, trendsetters, and honorable leaders.

The more we love ourselves and respect our limits, the more we *expand as people* and the more room we have in our hearts to be *altruistic*. Because of our own suffering and the deep love we have for life and people, we feel deeply inclined to share our success in any way we can. We feel inclined to give back through donating money or time to people, causes, or events. We donate a certain amount of our income believing that all we give out can only be returned to us tenfold. We do not entertain thoughts of lack. We have experienced the truth that there is enough for everyone. Knowing this from deep within our soul makes us unafraid and unselfish when giving of ourselves, financially and otherwise.

Most importantly, we strive to create *happiness* in others and to live happily ourselves. We discipline our minds, as we have come to understand the power our thoughts have over our emotions and our physical body. It is this awareness that allows us to learn from our thoughts and to choose thoughts and emotions that promote us and the happiness and success of others. For us happiness is not a given but rather a creation.

We have come to be *thankful for all of life*—for every ounce of the journey we have already traveled and thankful for the journey to continue forward into more success. Wherever there is gratitude, there is a spark of life. Wherever there is a spark of life, there is inspiration.

The more grateful you are for what you have, the more motivated it makes you to want to sustain and then elevate above your current level of success. Abundance is a beautiful thing. A great way to practice gratitude is to write "Thank you" on every check and every receipt as a way to remind yourself of how blessed you are to have the abundance to spend the money you spend.

When you are grateful, you become plentiful. The feeling of being abundant is inspiring because it is not a feeling you want to lose. You become more deeply committed to all you do when you treasure what you have. There is no room for complacency when you are grateful. Gratitude fills your heart and gives you an appreciation for all of life and for all those you love.

Because of this, you will feel ever inspired to create a new expansion-plan for your life. There is no ending to success or happiness because emotional wealth is not a destination. Emotional wealth is the chase, the journey, the desire to capture something more. It is that elusive quality of fulfillment and success that stirs your soul and inspires you to live, to dream, and to contribute.

MARINATE ON THIS

It is the chase, not the capture, that brings you the most satisfaction. It is this chase that cultivates the depth of your emotional wealth.

—*Dr. Sherrie Campbell*

Acknowledgments

I would like to extend my gratitude to the Morgan James family for giving me a shot at my publishing dreams.

I want to thank Terry Whalin for following me on Twitter and for being open to hearing about me and my writing. I felt something so special in you, and I knew that your interests in me were genuine. From the second we talked, I knew you were on my team. I will never forget getting your call telling me that Morgan James Publishing was offering me a contract.

I want to thank Bill Watkins, my incredible editor. I could not have been blessed with a better coach, guide, and partner to help make *Success Equations* into the book that it has grown to be. I am so proud of what we have accomplished together. I consider you to be such an important and special person in my life.

I want to thank my beautiful daughter, London. London, you are my angel and my Why in life. You are my greatest and deepest blessing.

I want to thank Scott Holmes for your unfaltering love and support.

I want to thank all of my friends and my chosen family for loving me and inspiring me every day to be the best version of myself that I can be.

I want to thank all of the people who have hurt me. The hurt you have inflicted into my life forced me to deeply find, know, accept, and love myself. I have risen and will continue to rise inspired by you. Because of the barriers you placed in my way, I have come to trust the depth of my spirit and the beautiful resilience I have within me to overcome.

231

About the Author

Dr. Sherrie Campbell is a nationally recognized expert in clinical psychology, an inspirational speaker, former radio host of the *Dr. Sherrie Show* for the BBM Global Network and TuneIn Radio, and an active writer for *Huffington Post* and Entrepreneur.com. Her blogs are seen in nearly all sections of the *Huffington Post*, and she's one of the top read contributors for Entrepreneur. com. Dr. Sherrie is also a regularly featured expert on radio and television with her most recent airing on *FOX 11 News*.

Dr. Sherrie was selected by the Beauty In Beauty Out Tour 2015 and received a Reflection Award in Los Angeles for being a Real Superwoman in her community. She received this award in acknowledgement for her dedication to freely providing love, support, advice, and motivation on her professional Facebook page (www.facebook.com/sherriecampbellphd). Fifteen elite women in the state of California were chosen for this acknowledgement. She is now a current board member for the Beauty In Beauty Out Foundation.

Dr. Sherrie earned her PhD in 2003 and is a licensed psychologist with over two decades of clinical training experience providing counseling and psychotherapy services to residents of Orange County in California. She not only works with patients in her private practice but also mentors and shares her expertise with others throughout the United States and worldwide, providing sessions via phone call or Facetime. In her private practice, she specializes in psychotherapy with adults and teenagers, including providing marriage and family therapy and counseling for grief, childhood trauma, sexual issues, personality disorders, illness, and more. Dr. Sherrie has helped individuals manage their highest highs and survive their lowest lows—from winning the lottery to the death of a child. Her interactive sessions are as unique and impactful as is her book, *Loving Yourself: The Mastery of Being Your Own Person.*

She is the mother of a daughter who inspires her every move in life. Dr. Sherrie is also an avid athlete, and she loves her alone time to read and write in her journal.

Morgan James
Speakers Group

www.TheMorganJamesSpeakersGroup.com

We connect Morgan James published
authors with live and online events
and audiences who will benefit
from their expertise.

Printed in the USA
CPSIA information can be obtained
at www.ICGtesting.com
JSHW022320140824
68134JS00019B/1213

9 781683 508878